W9-AZH-446

IF YOU DON'T
MAKE
WAVES
YOU'LL DROWN

10 Hard-Charging Strategies for
Leading in Politically Correct Times

Dave Anderson

WILEY

John Wiley & Sons, Inc.

Copyright © 2006 by John Wiley & Sons, Inc. All rights reserved.

Published by John Wiley & Sons, Inc., Hoboken, New Jersey.
Published simultaneously in Canada.

No part of this publication may be reproduced, stored in a retrieval system, or transmitted in any form
or by any means, electronic, mechanical, photocopying, recording, scanning, or otherwise, except as
permitted under Section 107 or 108 of the 1976 United States Copyright Act, without either the prior
written permission of the Publisher, or authorization through payment of the appropriate per-copy fee
to the Copyright Clearance Center, Inc., 222 Rosewood Drive, Danvers, MA 01923, (978) 750-8400,
fax (978) 646-8600, or on the web at www.copyright.com. Requests to the Publisher for permission
should be addressed to the Permissions Department, John Wiley & Sons, Inc., 111 River Street,
Hoboken, NJ 07030, (201) 748-6011, fax (201) 748-6008 or online at http://www.wiley.com/go/
permissions.

Limit of Liability/Disclaimer of Warranty: While the publisher and author have used their best efforts
in preparing this book, they make no representations or warranties with respect to the accuracy or
completeness of the contents of this book and specifically disclaim any implied warranties of
merchantability or fitness for a particular purpose. No warranty may be created or extended by sales
representatives or written sales materials. The advice and strategies contained herein may not be
suitable for your situation. You should consult with a professional where appropriate. Neither the
publisher nor author shall be liable for any loss of profit or any other commercial damages, including
but not limited to special, incidental, consequential, or other damages.

This publication is designed to provide accurate and authoritative information in regard to the subject
matter covered. It is sold with the understanding that the publisher is not engaged in rendering
professional services. If legal, accounting, medical, psychological or any other expert assistance is
required, the services of a competent professional person should be sought.

Designations used by companies to distinguish their products are often claimed as trademarks. In all
instances where John Wiley & Sons, Inc. is aware of a claim, the product names appear in initial
capital or all capital letters. Readers, however, should contact the appropriate companies for more
complete information regarding trademarks and registration.

For general information on our other products and services please contact our Customer Care
Department within the U.S. at (800) 762-2974, outside the United States at (317) 572-3993 or fax
(317) 572-4002.

Wiley also publishes its books in a variety of electronic formats. Some content that appears in print
may not be available in electronic books. For more information about Wiley products, visit our web
site at www.wiley.com.

ISBN-13: 978-0-471-72503-9 (cloth)
ISBN-10: 0-471-72503-X (cloth)

Printed in the United States of America.

10 9 8 7 6 5 4 3 2 1

This book is dedicated to Ashley:
The most caring, witty, bright, and beautiful daughter
a grumpy old dad could ever have the privilege of
loving and raising.

Contents

Preface

If you can make it through the Preface and Introduction of this book without throwing it across the room into a trash can, or angrily closing it for the last time, then number 1, I'd be very much obliged, and number 2, there is hope for you as a leader in the midst of today's politically correct climate. Let me explain:

It's a fact that society's trends influence business trends. As a result, the world's embrace of political correctness has infected the business world and diminished and debilitated the performance-based psyche required to build an elite organization. Like any unchecked disease, PC continues to spread, creating a too-tolerant cesspool in the workplace that drains morale and preempts results.

In bluntest terms, political correctness is dishonest. It sacrifices truth for the sake of harmony. Its objective—to offend no one and treat all equally—abuses stars while it subsidizes sluggards. Worse, politically correct leaders are prone to subordinate creativity to conformity and replace innovation with emulation, all the while weakening the strong to strengthen the weak.

If you assume a too-politically correct leadership style you will join a growing herd of sheep that leaves a mire of mediocrity in its wake, as you diminish your spirit with compromise and cowardice while you wrongly rationalize away what you know is right and true for what is expedient. "Political correctness" is more than a term. It's a dangerous state of mind and it is a trend. As a businessman, writer, speaker, and citizen, I'm alarmed by its reach and its depth in society and the workplace—and I think all productive people should be as well. In fact, the purpose of my book is to nudge, cajole, persuade, or push you up to a higher level of leadership that requires larger doses of tough love, higher expectations, and stronger accountability. It can be a painful journey, and things I say or suggest along the way may tick you off—but someday you'll thank me.

The bottom line is that *If You Don't Make Waves, You'll Drown* is written to arm you: to help you tighten up, toughen up, and step up to build a high-performance business culture in spite of today's politically correct stench. If you apply the Hard-Charging Strategies found in each chapter and adjust your style to fit these times you will not only survive but will earn an insanely unfair advantage for your organization. If instead you follow the PC fads that promote diversity over results, confuse loyalty with tenure, and fail to hold others accountable for their actions, you could become irrelevant as a leader and relegated to chief steward of an organizational outhouse. This descent has become all too common today, and I want you to personally avoid the plunge as well as to capitalize on those who fail to see the light and make the necessary adjustments: your competitors.

As I look around today, I am convinced that both society and the business world are in a heap of trouble. A recent generation of Americans has been rightly characterized as the "Greatest Generation." As political correctness in society and business compromises our values, sullies high standards, and supplants merit with entitlement, much of our population has devolved into the rationalization generation.

Things only get worse when otherwise good people complain about political correctness but do nothing to stop it. Business and social structures are used to weaken the strong and prop up the weak. And if you haven't yet recognized how society's "anything goes," "you're okay I'm okay," "let's show a little more tolerance" mantras of Milquetoast are invading and wilting the performance-based psyche necessary to run your business and obstructing the way you manage employees, then I highly recommend you pull your head out of wherever it's been hiding and deal with the world as it is rather than as you'd like it to be.

Society's trends to abandon standards, morals, and the acceptance of responsibility for one's life directly affects the mindset of you and your employees, and if you haven't previously given the correlation much thought; consider this as a friendly wake-up call. My ranting on about its evils may make you uncomfortable or even angry, but closing your eyes in denial only aids and abets its impact on your business and the society in which you live. The bottom line: Political correctness has gone too far. Its proliferation affects you, your children, your employees, and your business, and it's time to fight back.

Whether you head a small family firm burdened with spoiled, do-nothing offspring, a mammoth concern where the rank-and-file have become lazy and convinced themselves that tenure substitutes for results, or if you lead the ultra-successful who've become intoxicated with success and are convinced they've arrived, *If You Don't Make Waves, You'll Drown* offers the inspiration and hard-charging strategies to elevate your corporate welfare state to a meritocracy, or take an already good company and make it elite.

Make no mistake: Building a meritocracy is laborious while burdened with today's hypertolerance, "it's not my fault" losers' limps, and undisciplined workforce. But my guess is that you already work long and hard, that you care deeply about your business, and that you are up to the task. And if you're going to put forth a sincere effort each day to build a better life for your employees, your family, and yourself, you deserve to gain a greater return on your blood, sweat, and tears. But that means you'll have to make some waves while you're at work, because personal and corporate greatness will not just happen by doing more of what you've always done. In fact, the weakening effects of political correctness on culture, your employee's work ethic, and your own mindset can seduce you into doing the easy, cheap, popular, or convenient thing, rather than what's right—and often difficult. Just as has happened in society, politically correct pressures are causing business people to rationalize, trivialize, and marginalize the tough issues and to become disoriented to absolutes like right and wrong, success and failure, and winning and losing. On one hand, we're reluctant to give our best to the best, and on the other, we're afraid to fire the lazy, the lousy and the lost. We've become too reliant on consensus and prone to buy into the chorus that anything goes, that nothing is anyone's fault, and that outside conditions, not inside decisions, determine our fate. In the absence of accountability, political correctness creates a culture of entitlement that breeds mass mediocrity and saps passion from your best employees.

This doesn't have to happen to you. If it has, you can still win—but you can't prevail by presiding, administering, or simply managing your business; you're going to have to toughen up, make some waves, and lead it. Following is a blueprint from this book to help you divorce from the politically correct herd and become a tougher, tighter, leader, who lives and leads well in the midst of the PC sump:

Chapter 1: Don't Be a Wimp!
You can't lead effectively today if you're a wimp running around taking polls and trying to make everyone happy. You'll learn four key traits in this chapter that you must weave into your personal leadership style to optimize results.

Chapter 2: Send the Moochers Packing!
Entitlement is an offspring of political correctness. This chapter offers examples of the debilitating affects of entitlement on society and their subsequent trend to carry over into and impact your business, and teaches you to establish the polar opposite of a welfare state in your business: a meritocracy.

Chapter 3: Don't Confuse the Scoreboard for the Game!
Politically incorrect leaders don't get duped or seduced by the great results people produce: They look at *how* their people are getting the job done because the *how* is where these people are headed. In Chapter 3 you'll not only learn to keep "the numbers" in their proper perspective, but also how to become a more astute student of behaviors, culture, and disciplines—all keys to building and sustaining a meritocracy.

Chapter 4: Sometimes You Have to Tick People Off!
Honest feedback oftentimes hurts people's feelings and can make them mad—but that's a small price to pay to correct their course and edify the organization. This chapter teaches three types of feedback you must give quickly, consistently, and honestly in order to maintain a pressure to perform and bring the best out of your people, and two feedback strategies to avoid.

Chapter 5: Learn to Read between the Lies!
Politically incorrect leaders make waves by challenging conventional thinking and by refusing to instinctively follow the herd of best practices in business. This chapter offers three examples of how conventional wisdom hides the truth in both society and business, and teaches the importance of being more cynical of generally accepted dogmas, the government, the media, and most of the people you deal with.

Chapter 6: Ditch Diversity and Go for Results!
In politically correct organizations the pursuit of diversity supercedes the quest for results. However, diversity without competence is worthless! Chapter 6 coaches you on how to make waves and eliminate an Affirmative Action mindset in your business, where people benefit precisely because of who they are rather than what they've ever done, and to put merit and results in their proper place when building your business; far ahead of gender, ethnicity, or racial preferences.

Chapter 7: Don't Just Win . . . Run up the Score!
Politically incorrect leaders don't want their fair share of the market: They want more. They don't seek a level playing

field: They want it stacked as far in their favor as possible. But they know that to accomplish this they must maintain a killer instinct, and outwork, outsmart, and out-lead their competition. Chapter 7 teaches you how to beat the live-and-let-live, play-not-to-lose tendency of PC wimps, and to focus on winning big and winning often.

Chapter 8: Spare the Rod, Spoil the Sluggard!
If you want to change someone's behavior you must do more than give endless pep talks, cross your fingers, hold your breath, and hope something good happens. You must care enough about your people to make waves, to confront them when they veer off-track, and learn to coach with consequences. Chapter 8 will teach you to leverage consequences as a key to changing employee behavior and ensuring more consistent results from your team.

Chapter 9: Don't Make People Happy. . . . Make Them Better!
Politically incorrect leaders understand it is not their job to make people happy. Their job is to make them better, and once people get better, they tend to get happy—and if getting better doesn't make them happy then they're not worth having around. This chapter will teach the importance of making waves and earning respect, first, and popularity, second, if at all.

Chapter 10: Don't Trade Your Values for Valuables!
Politically incorrect leaders lead by personal example, not personal convenience. This chapter makes the unconventional case for using your business as a vehicle to support

causes and movements that reflect your values, and to leave the world better than you found it.

I believe that much of what's in *Waves* will make sense to you and you'll agree with it—and some you will not. So let's get this on the table up front: It's always okay to disagree. Just keep an open mind and realize that when you're feeling uncomfortable or even offended it's because you're being stretched, and that without discomfort and stretching you won't grow to your fullest potential as a person or a leader. In fact, I would wager that the passages that disturb you the most in any book you read have the most to teach you. Overall, the thoughts and strategies I'm presenting are a lot like grocery shopping: If you like them put them in the cart; if you don't, leave them on the shelf. But at least take a look and see if they make some sense and will work for you.

Here's reassuring news: Rather than simply whine about the depths of depravity PC has dunked us in, *Waves* provides tools for excelling in spite of it, bucking the timid trend and creating a significant edge for you as a leader. My guess is that if you're as exhausted and offended by the delusion and denial you see people living in as I believe you are, you won't mind seeing PC drawn and quartered before you. In fact, I suspect you will find it refreshing.

Acknowledgments

There are so many people that have to put up with my impatience, high demands, and stubbornness in order to see a project like this book through to completion, that in the name of being inclusive and politically correct I should list them all here. However, to prevent this from sounding like an award show acceptance speech garbled by some gushy, windbag Hollywood starlet, I will limit my thanks to the most important person behind this project and in my life; my wife and business partner, Rhonda.

Author's Note

I haven't written this book to humor you, entertain you, or tell you how great you are. I'm not saying it's not important that someone do this for you, but I'm not the guy. I am here to help you, and I've seen enough once-effective leaders neutered by politically correct posturing and positioning to know that more sweet-talking will only make things worse.

I also want to present my background, since, as a reader, you deserve to know so you can better understand and evaluate the strategies presented here. My writing and speaking style is quite blunt, because in order to help you become a better leader and build a more vital enterprise I would rather offend you by being direct than affront you with fluff. I am not an academic and have built my own business without having anything handed to me. I should also share that I fit much of the world's definition of all that's evil and wrong in society in that I am a male, Caucasian, Christian, conservative.

What this last sentence means is that my left-leaning friends who promote tolerance and open-mindedness will have a chance to practice what they preach while reading this book. And if you happen to share my gender, race, religion, or political persuasion and smugly assume that this book is designed to represent these aspects as superior, think again because we get our share wrong much of the time.

As I observe what is *not* working in the workplace or in the world overall, I would respectfully suggest that if people from all political affiliations, denominations, and religions would take the time, money, and energy they spend trying to prove they are right and the rest of the world is wrong and invest it in doing good then life would be a lot more pleasant for us all.

As you may have already discerned *If You Don't Make Waves, You'll Drown* is not your typical warm and fuzzy business manual. In fact, if you're not periodically uncomfortable while reading the book, I will have failed you. Admittedly, I even cross the line of propriety from time to time to make a point. You are more likely to find this book irritating than motivating, but that's a good thing, since frustration and dissatisfaction are unequalled motivators.

If you don't like the way I make my point or present a strategy, frankly, that's your privilege, but you must understand that I gave up trying to make everyone happy years ago, and it was one of the most liberating things I've ever done. In fact, throughout the book I'm going to try and convince you to do the same. I guess the bottom line is that if you want to be hugged and coddled by an author, you'll have to read someone else's book. Don't get me wrong: I care deeply about people. In fact, I care enough to confront them when they're off-track, to tell the truth even when it hurts, and to irritate them enough to get them to leave their comfort zone and grow.

If you continue to read *Waves* you have implicitly agreed to the terms disclosed. Because of this, you should know that I don't welcome negative comments, emails, phone calls, threats, or feedback about how I hurt your feelings, offended you, excluded you, or otherwise made you unhappy. Sorry, but life is too short. While I take shots at a handful of deserving public figures and professions and poke fun at certain backgrounds, my bottom-line business philosophy is simple: I don't care if you're a Christian, Jew, Hindu, Muslim, Buddhist, or deist; white, black, brown, yellow, green, purple, or pink; male, female, gay, straight, or confused, there are three elements that trump all these factors in leadership: character, competence, and consistency. Without these it is impossible to have the maniacal focus on results necessary to build an elite organization. I am biased and prejudiced against only three things: lack of character, lack of competence, and lack of consistency. I hope you find that fair. In fact, I encourage the same three prejudices—and only these three prejudices—among all business leaders.

A final word: Those of you that have read my prior books will notice I've taken it up a notch and presented an even more direct and bare-knuckles approach in *Waves*, because I believe many leaders are running out of time. They're heading for disaster. It's not that they don't want to fix their businesses; many of them are functionally blind to what is happening to their businesses. They don't see it and they just don't get it. They don't realize the urgency to toughen up and tighten up. They don't grasp that there is less margin for error.

Frankly, many people might benefit greatly from this book if, instead of reading it, a friend whacked them upside the head with it to help bring them to their senses more quickly than I can with mere words. If this is you, you'll realize it soon enough as you read through each chapter. From that point on you can no longer lean on the crutch of ignorance for failing to lead more effectively in politically correct times. After all, ignorance indicates that you don't know any better. Once you know better but still do unproductive things you must then assume the banner of stupidity. However, I say this without fear of offending you because I don't believe it relates to you: Even if it does, the fact that you read this far tells me you're tough enough to take it.

Introduction

Political correctness is defined as conforming to a belief that language and practices that could offend sensibilities as pertains to sex, race, or religion should be eliminated. In its purest form, this definition makes sense. Unfortunately, the definition of PC has swelled over the years, so that saying or doing anything offensive to someone—for any reason—is taboo. In fact, it could make you the defendant in a lawsuit or label you a racist or a bigot. As a result, political correctness has created an unofficial form of censorship in society and the workplace.

If you're the hypersensitive type this book will unsettle you, because it assails the values politically correct society may have seduced you into embracing. If, in fact, you are the hypersensitive type then you probably shouldn't have bought this book, because you may be so far gone over the politically correct edge that nothing can help you. Don't take this personally, because it doesn't mean you're a bad person: You're just a bad fit for the strategies in this book. Frankly, you probably won't like them.

So why would I risk turning off readers and perhaps alienating them in these early pages? Because in an age when we've become more concerned with not offending someone than we have in failing to tell the truth as we see it, we should consider this sad but brutal fact: There are droves of otherwise good people drown-

1

ing in denial, in both society and business, that need to wake up. Perhaps they even need offending—they need to hear the truth and to be shaken out of their delusion, because they're tiptoeing through life, talking, walking, and acting like victims. These people add value to nothing, and positively impact no one. Sorry if this sounds harsh. But just take a glance around you in the workplace and in society as a whole. My guess is that you won't have to look far or long to have this assertion validated.

The worst offenders are PC puppets in leadership positions: leadership wimps. These weak-sticks with titles have pledged allegiance to the status quo, sold out their values for valuables, are bereft of courage and immobilized by fear. Even worse, because they are "leaders," their spineless example has cascaded down throughout their organization, castrating the spirit of the rank and file, discouraging the talented at the top while at the same time creating a safe-house for bunglers at the bottom. If you are currently working for someone like this or have in the past, you know firsthand how infuriating these people are.

In my seminars, I ask audiences by a show of hands to indicate if they believe the world has become too politically correct. The answer is complete affirmation. I then ask if they believe that political correctness in society has the potential to negatively impact and influence the way they run their business and deal with their people. The answer, again, is an anthem of moans followed by a unanimous "Yes."

Quite frankly, you'd have to be living in a spider hole not to realize how out of hand the proliferation of politically correct doctrine has become, and to ignore the impact it has on your personal leadership style and your organization. But just in case you haven't been paying attention to society's drift toward political correctness the past few years, here are six examples of how trends in business follow trends in politically correct society—and the devastating impact this has on your enterprise. Be warned that some of these examples may seem unkind or a bit harsh, but if I'm going to encourage you to make waves, I need to walk my talk and do the same. So here goes:

Political Correctness Gone Nuts Example #1: Advocacy groups admonish governments and citizens to adjust their culture, values, and laws to accommodate growing populations of immigrants. While the vast majority of immigrants in this country make positive contributions, and many out-hustle and run circles around the home-grown team of citizens, the philosophy that a society should have to change to accommodate them is 100 percent backward. Undoubtedly, it is an immigrant's obligation to adapt to a country, not vice versa. And this assimilation should include learning to speak the language. If immigrants don't feel they can adjust to the country to which they immigrate and put its interests first they should stay put, and save everyone the headache of tolerating their insolence and being burdened by their ignorance.

The Impact on Business: Employees in today's workplace don't want to stretch to your expectations or live your workplace values— they want you to adjust and lower the bar to accommodate them. Today we live in an instant gratification society where people want the prize with little regard for paying the price—and they want it yesterday. People project a lottery mindset, hoping today is the day their number comes up, and seek fame and fortune without virtue of accomplishment. You witness a quota mentality, where people get a job or promotion because of what they are rather than what they've done; where genetics trumps merit, and the pursuit of diversity supercedes the quest for results. And you see spoiled whiners who believe they should get more money and promotions based on tenure, experience, and credentials rather than completing a simple task like getting the job done. This air of entitlement and arrogance can have only one outcome: the weakening and compromising of your enterprise.

Political Correctness Gone Nuts Example #2: School systems worldwide have experimented with eliminating failing grades and competitive sports so students don't have to face failure and lose their self-esteem. These very students will be in for a rude awakening the moment they join a merit-based company and discover that there are absolutes like winning and losing, succeeding and failing, and right and wrong. In the meanwhile, politically correct school administrators, influenced by the advocates for underachievers at the National Education Association, are breeding a generation of victims and whiners that will don a "deer caught in headlights" stare once they graduate from their state-sanctioned institutions of underachievement and have to get a real job. In fact, you may already have some of these deadbeats cashing your paychecks. Well, just wait, because you ain't seen nothing yet. With society's rapid trend toward even more tolerance and less competition, it's going to get worse.

The Impact on Business: As you look at businesses today you see leadership lightweights failing to hold subordinates accountable because they fear offending them. These morons with management monikers choose harmony over truth and lower their standards to accommodate deadweights rather than stretch people to attain their high standards. Leaders conduct sugarcoated employee reviews rather than tell people they're failing. They're afraid to fire the timorous, the tepid, and the trite; they give six second chances to the marginal, mediocre, and moronic, and appoint themselves public defender of the dismal, the derelict, and the depressed. These behaviors betray and demoralize your best people, as they become diminished and cheapened while having to share the workplace with a thundering herd of jackasses. These actions completely devastate the high performance, merit-based culture necessary to build an elite organization.

Political Correctness Gone Nuts Example #3: Prodded on by the anti-God, high-profile ambulance chasers at the ACLU (American Civil Liberties Union), judicial activists order the removal of nativity scenes and religious symbols from public property because of their potential to offend. This judicial "stench from the bench" does so under the auspices of separation of church and state, even though this phrase doesn't appear in our Constitution: It is a modern manifestation of political correctness gone berserk. Perhaps some day atheist jurists will get back to interpreting the law rather than reinventing it in the name of political correctness.

The Impact on Your Business: The business arena today is filled with leadership amateurs choosing to do what's easy rather than what's effective. They surrender what the majority wants, needs, and supports in order to accommodate a chorus of whining, wimpy, "victikrats." The tendency to back down and elevate the cause of malcontents rather than putting the good of the team ahead of any one individual's hurt feelings or sense of isolation causes the leaders to stand for nothing, fall for everything, and lose respect and credibility as they become despised by top performers.

Political Correctness Gone Nuts Example #4: Students at universities are asked not to flaunt the national flag or sing patriotic songs at sporting events because of the potential to offend and isolate international students. However, if these foreign guests would read our Constitution rather than come here to trample on it they would see that there is nothing in it that guarantees anyone the right not to be offended, and if they ever feel too abused by nationalistic fervor they can exercise our country's greatest liberty— which is the freedom to leave it and go back to the Eden they escaped to come and annoy us.

The Impact on Your Business: Increasingly, leaders believe they have to be everything to everyone rather than do what's best for the team overall. They spend 80 percent of their time with the bottom 20 percent of their performers, engaging in rescue missions to elevate the miserable to mediocre rather than reward and support the top 20 percent who have earned it. And they resist doing anything special for top performers, embracing the socialistic mantra, "If I do it for him or her, I'd have to do it for everyone." Thus, so as not to offend, the bar is dropped low enough so the sluggards can clear it—resulting in a corporate communism that assures abuse of valuable resources and ensures a bottom line on a starvation diet.

Political Correctness Gone Nuts Example #5: World leaders, reluctant to make tough decisions, look to the United Nations to solve their problems. However, there is a reason no one has yet written a book titled, "How to Run Your Business Like the United Nations." In the United Nations, wealthy countries (the productive) are increasingly admonished and resented for being prosperous and powerful, and are implored to give more freebies to developing nations (the unproductive) in order to level the economic playing field.

6

This happens in spite of the fact that since World War II the United States alone has given over two trillion dollars in foreign aid.

In the process of turning much of the world into a welfare state the benefactor countries have created an alarming sense of entitlement, so that whatever they do for one of these struggling, stone-age states is never enough. The U.N. has become the epitome of PC nonsense, as it is headed mostly by third world bureaucrats intent on helping nonproductive entities become bigger misfits and moochers—courtesy of Western handouts. How does this management philosophy affect your business? Take a look.

The Impact on Your Business: Incredibly, some businesses today seem to be adopting the United Nations style of management. They pursue diversity instead of results, rob the strong to help the weak, discuss but don't decide, and work overtime to make sure everyone is happy and in harmony. This emulation is a death wish, because the U.N. is one of the least effective organizations in the world, competency-challenged to stop a food fight at scout camp.

As a result of the "give me something for nothing" mentality pervasive in society, here's what you find trending in today's workplace: Employees have become more entitled than ever before, and are focused far more on what they think they are owed than what they owe—putting forth minimal effort and expecting maximum return. They increasingly ask what more will be done for them—and whatever you do is never enough. Entitled workers enlist en masse into the "just enough" club in the workplace. They do just enough to get by; just enough to pay their bills; just enough to not get fired. These slouches believe that loyalty should be measured by the amount of time they put into a company rather than by what they actually put into the time. They seek kudos for show-ing up rather than for stepping up.

Political Correctness Gone Nuts Example #6: This one is going to stir the pot, but it needs to be said. I'll delve more deeply into the is-sue in Chapter Six, but for now let me open the door to a perva-sive problem that is worsening as you read this.

Professional agitators advocate a persistently vile brand of race-based victimhood that encourages a welfare mentality and projects a racist worldview onto an entire class of people, inviting them to be angry and blameful rather than teaching them how to be successful in life. These self-appointed leaders, who teach that programs rather than principles are the keys to prosperity, become personally wealthy through agitation, protest, and corporate blackmail, while the constituency they denigrate with their rep-resentation becomes more desperate and indigent as they drink the "it's not my fault, you owe me more, give me another some-thing-for-nothing" Kool-Aid brewed by these shameless and morally impoverished kooks.

What a disgrace. In less than 40 years the civil rights move-ment has gone from the incredible leadership of Dr. King, a pro-ponent of merit-based achievement, to shakedown artists and riot kings. The droves of successful African Americans that have abro-gated the anger and blame, "I'm a victim" poison pontificated by this brood deserve special acclaim, while the many who rejoice in the absolution of responsibility for their lives are complicit in their own demise.

The Impact on Your Business: In many politically correct workplaces today the pursuit of diversity supercedes the quest for results. People are hired and promoted because of who they are rather than because they are best for the job. And an entire generation of supervisors is reluctant to disagree with, criticize, hold accountable, redirect, or terminate nonperforming minorities for fear of being labeled a racist, or waking up one day to find a racial agitator leading his mob-for-hire protesting outside their workplace, spewing "we're a victim" verses.

Society's "you're a victim because you're a minority" mantra also encourages a sense of martyrdom from those who are passed over for promotions, as they lament it was because of their color, gender, ethnic origin, or religion.

When workplace issues that are clear matters of right versus wrong are twisted into matters of black versus white, business leaders, paralyzed by fear, opt to do what is cheap, easy, convenient, and popular, rather than what is just. This business version of affirmative action and the subsequent creation of corporate welfare states resolutely destroys the strongest of merit-based, high-performance business cultures. It's simply a matter of time. In fact, it may be debilitating yours as you read these words.

I could continue ad nauseam, but the crisis is clear, and it's enough to make society's competent and deserving lose their heart, their morale, and their lunch. I used to think political correctness was a fad or a trend that would fizzle over time, but I'm sickened to see it sinking its roots deeper into society's psyche, with its residual affect on business cultures and leadership mindsets no less than crippling. As political correctness amplifies its hold on business you must tighten up, toughen up, step up, and adapt your leadership style to confront and correct its assault.

The hard-charging strategies in *If You Don't Make Waves, You'll Drown* provide the impetus to accomplish precisely this task. Before you look too long at outside conditions or at the deficiencies of those who share your workplace, look first in the mirror. Effective leaders are always looking for ways to improve their own leadership style to fit the times, the situation, and the person. In fact, commit to make this the year you work harder on your own leadership development than ever before. It's never been more important. Only as you personally tighten up and toughen up will you have the credibility, confidence, and competence to positively impact your organization amidst the minefield created by this politically correct era.

While the examples I offer of political correctness gone nuts hail mainly from the United States, I have no doubt that my readers in Canada, the United Kingdom, Europe, Australia, Asia, and beyond will easily be able to relate to similar nonsense in their own countries. In fact, when you run across examples of PC gone nuts, I'd love to hear about them. Email them to pcgonenuts@ learntolead.com and you just might find them in my next book.

CHAPTER

1

Don't Be a Wimp!

Peering into the PC Cesspool

WCMH-TV in Ohio reported that Glendening Elementary School, in Grovesport, has banned celebrations of Halloween, Christmas, and Valentine's Day, in part because a few deprived students don't participate in these holidays due to their personal beliefs. The kids at this gulag will no longer be able to play dress-up, eat candy canes, or exchange valentines because goose-stepping killjoys say they need the extra few hours a year spent in these parties to improve academic results.

Furthermore, they've also eliminated individual birthday parties in favor of one big birthday orgy, where everyone's special day will be celebrated. If the wimpy wardens at this elementary prison were truly interested in improving grades they'd support rather than oppose teacher competency testing, and hold their weak-stick teachers to a higher standard. These kids don't need more hours of schoolwork to improve their grades—they need more competent teachers who can do their job and who aren't allowed to hide their inadequacy behind tenure or their union.

Business Lesson: Today's school systems are breeding a generation of future workplace wimps who will be ashamed of their unique abilities, maintain no sense of competitive spirit, and grow up believing it's okay to put the needs of a few whiners ahead of what's good for the majority. Unfortunately, many caring and competent teachers and bright students suffer under this oppressive system of lowering the bar to accommodate the few. By the time many of these under-achieving students enter and infect the workforce they'll be next to worthless, and little you can do will rehabilitate their politically correct illness.

You are well advised to take good care of the employees you already have and talk them into a long career with your organization, because if something doesn't change to re-kindle the merit-based, competitive spirit that once symbol-ized our school systems, much of this future crop of kids won't be worth hiring. In the meanwhile, if you have children of your own, here are five words of advice to help better pre-pare them for the real world: private schools or home school.

Defining the Wimps

Wimps are defined by the *Oxford Dictionary* as weak, feeble, or ineffectual people. Leadership wimps are those whose feeble and ineffectual style has caused them to assume a "too-tolerant, anything goes, everyone is beautiful, tell 'em what they want to hear, let's not rock the boat" leadership philosophy. This leadership style finds a welcome host in po-litically correct times. Yet it is terminal for any leader who is serious about getting sustainable results in today's business climate. If you or your employees have it you'll need to ditch it fast, and assume more of the four traits promoted in this chapter.

A key differentiator between average and effective lead-ers is the ability to adapt their leadership style to fit the indi-vidual, the circumstances, and the times. Adapting your leadership style doesn't mean you try to become someone you are not, although some leaders are so inept that becoming someone else would probably save their career.

What adapting your style *does* mean is leveraging the most relevant traits and practices necessary to get results in today's PC climate, and doing so more often. In most cases this will mean dispensing bigger doses of accountability and tough love.

Examine the following four traits of politically incorrect leaders. Consider which adjustments you should make in your leadership style in order to maximize outcomes in a politically correct cesspit that insists that you get fast results but mandates that you produce them with kid gloves and within the parameters of PC protocol.

Trait One: Politically Incorrect Leaders Discriminate

Discriminate? Yes, discriminate. I'm not advocating discrimination according to race, gender, or ethnicity. Instead, politically incorrect leaders discriminate in favor of talent, work ethic, and results, and discriminate against laziness, complacency, and mediocrity. This type of discrimination is not illegal. In fact, it's quite necessary to build an elite organization. And as offensive as this will sound to society's advocates for misfits and dullards; politically incorrect leaders give their best to the best and less to the rest. They understand that in a meritocracy, treating everyone fairly doesn't mean you treat them all alike; treating people fairly means you treat them in a manner they have earned and deserve based on past performance; they haven't all earned, nor do they deserve, the same discretion, opportunities, resources, amount of your time, work schedules, or compensation.

In a meritocracy, fairness doesn't mean sameness; fairness means justice, and justice means giving people what they earn and deserve. In fact, the only people in your business who might have a problem getting strictly what they earn and deserve are the slugs who haven't earned and don't deserve much. And if these vagrants get mad enough about your distribution of resources they might just really make your day and quit, saving you the trouble of firing them.

If the last sentence appears brutal, please remember that this book is not designed as therapy or amusement. It's written to equip you to maximize your leadership results and perhaps save your job or your company in the process. Your mission is to get better and to lead at a higher level. Your job is to either get your people better or get better people, and if you don't get or can't accept or execute this basic yet vital principle, you shouldn't be in a leadership position. Don't take it personally; this doesn't mean you're a bad person. It simply means you're unfit to run a lemonade stand. I'm aware the last sentence or two haven't been very motivating. This is because my time is better spent irritating you into action than trying to sweet talk you into it. Sorry, but desperate times call for desperate measures.

Following are three examples of how leaders and organizations used discrimination to maximize results:

A. Jesus: The easiest question I am asked in seminars or interviews is, "Who do you believe was the greatest leader of all time?" The answer is—Jesus. If this answer offends you for any reason, lighten up and look at the facts. What He accomplished in just three years of ministry, without official power or title, is without equal. He built a team, lead by example, and walked His talk. He created clarity and vision, exemplified straight talk and accountability, displayed a servant's attitude and intense sense of humility, all the while staying engaged in the trenches, avoiding perks and privilege that traditionally come with such acclaim. He also discriminated.

While Jesus had a primary team of twelve, He didn't spend equal time or energy with all. He invested most heavily in three: John, James, and Peter. The Bible reports that when Jesus ascended the mountain to be transfigured He didn't bring the whole team. He chose these three to accompany Him. He wasn't worried about offending the other nine. He brought the same three on special healing missions and into a secluded part of the Garden of Gethsemane to pray with Him the night of His arrest. From the cross, He gave John and His mother responsibility for one another.

After the Resurrection, Jesus gave Peter special attention and let him redeem his denial. The result of focusing on His highest potential disciples is as follows: James pioneered Christianity in Spain, and preached so boldly and effectively when he returned to Jerusalem that he was the first disciple martyred. John preached tirelessly, wrote one of the four Gospels, the book of Revelation, and three letters of the New Testament. A resurgent Peter helped validate and assimilate Paul into the Christian movement, preached the breakthrough sermon at Pentecost, helped bring Christianity to the Gentiles, and wrote two New Testament letters. Peter's own disciple, Mark, wrote another of the Gospels.

Jesus knew He had but a short time to make His mark and build the team that would establish His church after His death. He chose and invested most heavily in an inner circle of three to catalyze the mission. For this He didn't need to explain Himself or apologize. He did what was right and not what would have been more acceptable to the group.

B. Jack Welch. Jack Welch was chairman of General Electric for 20 years. While he led GE to explosive heights he set high expectations, gave brutally honest feedback, held people accountable for results, and developed leaders at all levels. He also discriminated. Not only did Welch invest exhaustively in the development of GE's high potentials, he also fired the bottom 10 percent of performers annually. Welch didn't suffer fools or bottom-dwellers for long. He knew their mediocrity would infect GE's culture, diminish their standards, lower morale, break momentum, and impair his own credibility.

When you worked for Welch you knew where you stood: If you stunk you knew it, and if you were great you knew that as well, and were treated accordingly. It doesn't get any fairer than that.

C. Frequent-buyer programs. Programs like airline frequent flyer clubs are examples of merit-based discrimination. Not all customers are treated alike. It doesn't matter which race, gender, or ethnic background you possess, the rules are simple: Those who spend the most money get preferred check-in, first class upgrade privileges, and free trips as a reward for their performance. Hotels use the same strategy. The more often you stay with them the higher your level of preferred status. In return you earn late checkouts, free upgrades to suites, and complementary nights, among other perks.

The once-a-year traveler is not going to get the same treatment at a Marriott or Hilton as the customer who routinely does business with either company. And that's exactly as it should be. Interestingly, you hear few complaints concerning the discrimination that corporations bestow favor upon their best customers, but whiners in the workplace squawk when their own bosses project the "give your best to the best" strategy to enrich top performers. Yet the same philosophy is at the root of each approach. After all, both groups, frequent buyers and top performers, add more value and put more dollars into the organization's coffers. Discrimination is both appropriate and necessary to advance the enterprise.

Hard-Charging Strategies

Someone once said that people are your greatest asset. That someone didn't tell the whole story. People are not your greatest asset; the right people are. The wrong people are your greatest catastrophe, and mediocre people are your greatest drain on resources. Bearing this in mind, consider the following:

1. You will never build a great organization around marginal people. Working with weak people drains you.

Investing in weakness at the expense of leveraging strength breaks your momentum, lowers morale, and misuses resources. It causes you to play endless games of catch-up.

Some of the people you're retaining shouldn't be on board in the first place, because they're just plain bad at what they do. And even if you manage to invert bad you don't get good: You just get not bad, and how far do you think you can take your organization with a troupe of "not bad" bunglers? It's time to face reality about your people and to stop seeing them as you'd like them to be. Some of them have too far to go. They're failing, and even if you improve them the opposite of failing is not excellent; it's merely passing. And as I recall, passing grades in schools started with a D–, and you rarely, if ever, bring a D– up to an A. The lesson? You cannot build an elite company if you spend priority time with problem people. Instead, you must spend priority time with "potential" people. Otherwise it's like going to a horse race and betting your life savings on a nag, just to improve its self-image; seemingly noble but ultimately stupid.

2. In the midst of PC times it takes courage to discriminate. Do you have it? If not, you had better find it. When you clearly define up front what you stand for and what you expect, and hold people accountable for their actions, you needn't worry about shyster blowhards coming by with a news crew to accuse you of discrimination in order to blackmail you to fund their hypocritical lifestyle. Why? Because you'll be engaging in ethical discrimination: absolutely legal and necessary.

As a politically incorrect leader you have an obligation to invest your time and resources where you receive the greatest return. You can't afford to try and be everything to everyone and shouldn't waste your time trying to make everyone happy. Not only is this impossible, it's not important. Get people better and then they'll get happy. And if getting better doesn't make them happy, get some real help.

Trait Two: Politically Incorrect Leaders Blow Up the Box

President Kennedy once said, "Conformity is the jailer of freedom and the enemy of growth." Business leaders should pay heed to his words. Rather than follow the herd, get out front and leave footprints. Don't just optimize; innovate, and take the risks necessary to gain an edge on your competitors.

When you blow up the box you'll make mistakes, but take solace in knowing that going 7 for 10 is better for your business than going 3 for 3, because if you're going 3 for 3 you're playing it too safe. You're so busy grabbing the low-hanging fruit that while you may not make many errors, neither will you have a breakthrough.

In a world enamored with "best practices," resist conventional thinking and consider it the realm of wimpy and obsequious followers; the unthinking, expendable sheep that live their lives by seeing a moving line and getting in it rather than thinking for themselves. The annals of business and history are filled with gutsy leaders who blew up the box, created an edge, won it all, and left mere scraps for the play-it-safe, politically correct laggards to fight over. They lived as Thoreau declared: "If a man does not keep pace with his companions, perhaps it is because he hears a different drummer. Let him step to the music which he hears, however measured or far away." The following politically incorrect leaders not only heard a different drummer, they turned the orchestra upside down.

A. *Ronald Reagan.* For 40 years, conventional wisdom said no country could win the Cold War. President Reagan disagreed. Employing an uncommon blend of optimism and determination he defied his opposition, played to win, and demonstrated that 40 years of stinking thinking could be overcome by a leader who rejected conventional poppycock, raised his sights, lived his convictions, and didn't blink when things got tough.

B. *Herb Brooks.* Conventional wisdom said that the students comprising the 1980 U.S. Olympic hockey team could never compete in the Olympics, much less win against the Soviets, who happened to be the best team in the world. U.S. coach Herb Brooks disagreed and decided to make waves. He reinvented the team's conventional philosophy, work ethic, and playbook, and then whipped the world at Lake Placid, winning a gold medal and sending his detractors and doubters home to ponder their miscalculations. Those who lived during this time will never forget the incredible lift and pride this victory brought Americans, as we agonized under economic malaise and our citizens were held hostage in Tehran.

C. *John Wooden.* Conventional wisdom deemed it impossible to win seven consecutive championships in any sport. Yet, John Wooden led the UCLA men's basketball team to reach this unequaled streak, and went on to win 10 national championships in 12 years. He worked in relative obscurity at UCLA as a coach for 15 years, refining his unconventional practice systems and coaching philosophy, mastering vital recruiting strategies before launching onto the scene and winning his first championship in 1964. And he did so without recruiting violations, without throwing chairs or belittling players.

D. *Abraham Lincoln.* Conventional wisdom says you could never have a nervous breakdown, suffer two business failures, and lose numerous elections and still be elected President of the United States. Abraham Lincoln persevered and became one of the greatest leaders in world history by leveraging politically incorrect leadership at one of America's most crucial moments. His detractors called him an ape and unworthy of being president. He didn't look like a president, sound like a president, or have a pedigree. But today the entire world knows Lincoln, while his severest critics sleep in graves of anonymity.

E. *Mel Gibson.* Conventional wisdom says you'd have to be crazy to spend 25 million dollars of your own money to produce and distribute a movie every major Hollywood studio turned down—and then spend another 25 million of your own funds to publicize it; especially if the movie is in Latin and Aramaic and violently portrays the crucifixion of Jesus, polarizing Hollywood, Jewish activists, and the secular establishment. But Mel Gibson heard the beat of a heavenly drummer, put his money and convictions where his mouth was, thumbed his nose at Hollywood's conventional thinking, faded the heat, silenced his critics, and stunned the world as *The Passion of Christ* raked in over $600 million dollars and became the ninth-highest grossing movie of all time. Even with all the bleeding heart hype that promoted Michael Moore's masterpiece of misdirection, *Farenheit 911*, five times as many people saw *The Passion of Christ!* If you were paying attention, this disparity portended the 2004 presidential election results.

Hard-Charging Strategies

To evaluate your leadership in the areas pointed out in this section, answer the following:

1. Have you become so conditioned by precedent that you have a difficult time thinking in the box, much less stepping outside of it? When is the last time you tried something for the first time?

2. Is innovation welcome in your organization, or is the premium placed on being right so strong that no one dares think bold and new? What differentiates you from your competition? If you can't be specific, you're in trouble—because without differentiation the only tool you'll have to earn a client's business is the lowest price. Whereas the more you differentiate, the less price sensitive people become.

3. What industry dogmas have you challenged lately? In most industries everyone looks at the same things and ignores the same things: What makes you different?

4. What dream or strategy is buried inside you because you fear failure? Do you understand that most people go to the grave with their best music still in them—and that when they die it is as though they never lived? You must do better. Politically incorrect leaders take a stand, determine to stand for something great, and identify what they're no longer willing to stand for.

5. Do you resist the need to have large numbers of people endorse your dreams? After all, most people live average lives at best, so why worry about what they think? In fact, most don't think at all. They just bob their head to whatever palaver they hear that best validates their own mindset and character. If you've done your homework, have summoned the conviction, and are willing to pay the price and see your dream through, then get moving. In the words of Goethe, "Whatever you can do or dream you can, begin it. Boldness has genius power and magic in it."

In today's politically correct climate Goethe would have had to write: "Whatever you can do or dream, be sure it doesn't offend anyone else or hurt their self-esteem, and then ask all your friends to vote on it, and if they can't decide, take it to the geniuses at the U.N., where it will meet death by delay."

Trait Three: Politically Incorrect Leaders Hold Others Accountable for Results

Holding people accountable for results doesn't mean you have to yell, demean, belittle, or disrespect others. In fact, if you do these things you deserve a politically incorrect beating. Your efforts are much more effective when you explain your expectations and the ensuing consequences for failure clearly, firmly, and respectfully. Being direct is not an excuse for being a jerk or inflicting abuse.

Accountability Rule #1: Start with yourself. Before you can even think about holding others accountable, you must walk your own talk and assume responsibility for your personal results—or lack of results. In other words, suck it up and look in the mirror first before you look out the window and try to fix the rest of the world. Accept responsibility. Admit your mistakes. Hold yourself to a higher standard. Don't be a hypocrite. Adulterers don't give fidelity lectures. The French don't conduct courage clinics and the Enron crooks don't write on ethics.

Rudy Giuliani nailed the essence of self-accountability when he said: "I don't deserve all the credit I received for what went right while I was mayor, or all the blame for what went wrong, but I do deserve to be held accountable for the results of my office." Rudy Giuliani's quote doesn't tell the whole story concerning his leadership philosophy. On his desk was a sign: "I am responsible." The same goes for you so put away your black belt in blame when things turn south.

Accountability Rule #2: A second aspect of accountability is clarity. Many leaders do a poor job with accountability because they don't set clear performance and behavioral expectations up front. Thus, they have no benchmark for accountability. After all, ambiguity is the enemy of accountability.

If you don't take the time to create clarity you can't make the time to effectively hold others accountable. Do you have clear performance and behavioral expectations in your workplace? If not, quit being lazy, put your thinking cap on and decide what you're willing to stand for and what you're not willing to fall for. Then communicate these expectations so clearly and often that you take away all excuses of ignorance from your people: "I didn't know that's what you wanted," "I wasn't sure that was what you meant," "I didn't realize that's what you expected," and the like. Following is a list of what I refer to as the Business Facts of Life. As you consider these twenty-five politically incorrect expectations, determine how many of them are relevant to creating the clarity you need in your business. Use these Facts of Life as a catalyst to creating a clear benchmark of expectations in your business.

The Business Facts of Life

1. It's okay not to like a part of your job but it's not okay not to do it. In fact, I don't expect you to like everything about your job. That's why we pay you to do it. If you loved everything about your job we'd have to turn the workplace into an amusement park and charge you admission for being here.

2. Everyone on this team has a voice, but that doesn't mean you get a vote. This is not a democracy. I will listen, but I will also decide.

3. Everyone will be held to the same high standard of work ethic, customer care, and character. Beyond that, I will treat you in a manner you have earned and deserve and will invest my time and resources accordingly. I will give

my best to the best and less to the rest. I will run a meritocracy, not a welfare state.

4. You are expected to prove yourself over again every day. Tenure, credentials, and years of experience don't substitute for results. No one is paying you to pace yourself or budget your efforts.

5. I will work with you as long as you continue to make measurable progress in reasonable time. However, if you reach a point where you hover at or below average performance levels with no upward trend, I will lose interest in you. I do not endeavor to become a savior of lost causes or immerse myself in endless rescue missions.

6. I not only expect you to work hard on the job, I expect you to work hard on yourself. If you don't grow, you go. The day you stop bringing something of value to the table is the day I no longer have use for you.

7. My pay plan, bonuses, and incentive programs will reward above-average performers and above-average results, only. I will not subsidize or legitimize mediocrity by rewarding unworthy performances.

8. When promotions are available, they will go to the most qualified member of the team, regardless of longevity, gender, or ethnic background. I'm running a business, not a Royal Family. I have created an environment hostile to an affirmative action mindset. If the most qualified candidate for promotion is a white, Anglo-Saxon, Protestant male, he will get the job. On the other hand, if it is a physically challenged woman of color, the job goes to her.

9. I expect you to focus on what you can control; never assume a martyr's mindset to explain away your lack of success. Regardless of outside conditions, your inside decisions will determine your success. Even in the worst of times you can control your attitude, your discipline, and your character choices, and I will expect you to do so.

10. I measure loyalty by performance, not the number of years you cash my paychecks. The most disloyal thing you can do is to stop getting results. Loyalty is not the amount of time you put in; it's what you put into the time.

11. I will give you prompt, consistent, and brutally honest feedback on performance. If you are great, I will tell you. If you are failing, I will tell you. If you are ever unsure of where you stand, ask me.

12. I expect you to choose the truth over harmony. Make the right decision, not the cheap, popular, easy, or convenient one.

13. You are to lead your people deliberately and avoid doing what comes naturally. If you are having a bad day, suck it up and bear it. Don't put it on your sleeve and wear it or share it. Since everyone you work with has their own problems there is no need to share yours.

14. I will train you and invest in your development, but I also expect you to invest in yourself. In fact, if you don't invest in yourself, why should anyone else?

15. I expect you to lead by personal example, not personal convenience. This means you must commit yourself to a cause and not commit the cause to yourself. The day

you put your personal agenda ahead of the teams' is the day you must leave my organization.

16. If you lie, cheat, or steal I will fire you. There will be no second warning.

17. I expect you to add value to others on your team. Be a giver and not just a taker. If you are in it just for yourself you're in a mighty small business.

18. When dealing with others I expect you to practice one rule: the Golden Rule. This is not an option.

19. If you have personal problems that affect your work, I will listen, advise, and try to help you. However, you are expected to work through the paradox of solving your personal problems while you continue to get results on the job. Personal problems should not be construed as license for an indefinite production holiday.

20. I expect you to become brilliant in the basics of your job. You don't have to do anything extraordinary on a daily basis. Just do the ordinary things extraordinarily well.

21. I expect you to learn from mistakes and continue to take shots, even when you miss. When you hit a wall, learn to bounce, don't splatter.

22. I expect you to avoid repeating the same mistakes. While mistakes are a good investment when you learn from them, repeating the same ones evinces a carelessness that I will not tolerate.

23. I expect you to become an "and then some" person. Do what is required and then some. Hit your numbers and then some. Keep your promise and then some.

24. Don't whine, gossip, or complain on my time.

25. I don't tolerate skunks that make the numbers. Thus, I will measure you by two metrics: performance expectations and behavioral expectations. Not only do I expect you to perform the technical part of your job well, I expect you to share the company core values. If you make the numbers but don't live the values you are expendable.

It has been said that the first responsibility of a leader is to define reality. That's exactly what the business facts of life accomplish in your organization. They lift the fog off your expectations and provide a benchmark for accountability which is vital when you build a meritocracy. After all, it's hard for your people to be aggressive when they are confused about what you expect. Defining clear expectations takes the emotion out of having to deal with offenders later, because you made what was expected quite clear.

There are two key reasons leaders fail to create clarity for their organization: laziness and cowardice. Laziness explains itself, but by cowardice I mean that politically correct leadership wimps who'd rather be well liked and popular than hold people accountable for results don't create clarity, because they know if they never lay on the line exactly what they want there won't be as much pressure on them to confront the wrong behaviors when they manifest.

Three Lessons in Politically Incorrect Accountability

1. During the Civil War, Abraham Lincoln proved an ideal boss. Humble yet decisive, driven while support-

ive, he laid out clear expectations for his generals and then got out of their way. However, he did not bond with blunderers for long. In the 3-year period from the war's inception until the appointment of Ulysses S. Grant as General in Chief, Lincoln fired, demoted, or reassigned six key generals due to their inability to get results.[1] These pompous, incompetent knuckleheads were responsible for the loss of thousands of lives. Lincoln didn't let public opinion sway his resolve to do what was right. Some of the men he removed or sidelined were popular with the public and with the troops—they simply couldn't deliver the knockout punch to a vastly outmanned Confederate force.

Lincoln cared only for one thing: victory. He wasn't attached to sentimentalism, beholden to tradition, or affected by petty politics. What a contrast to modern-day political putzes, who spend more time polishing their soiled image and lying until our senses dull rather than making the tough decisions necessary to make a difference. No leader in American history has had to lead under such trying circumstances as did Lincoln. Ten days before he took the oath of office in 1861 the future Confederate States of America seceded from the Union.[2] To worsen matters, Lincoln was elected by a minority of the public vote, and was viewed by his own advisors as a geeky bumpkin with no leadership experience.

Opponents were mistaken to confuse his gawkiness for weakness. This leader meant business and cared not whether he was liked or hated. He held himself accountable, spending more days out of the White House during the Civil War than he did inside, as he visited generals at battlefields on numerous occasions to gain first-hand knowledge and make a personal impact on his subordinates, personally coming under sniper fire at Ft. Stevens in Silver Spring, Maryland, while surveying Confederate troops.[3]

2. UCLA men's basketball coach John Wooden was on his way to leading the Bruins to a 30–0 season and their first of 10 national championships in 1964. In the final game of the season, after having a brilliant year, center Fred Slaughter was playing an awful game. In fact, as time progressed he went from bad to worse. Shunning sentimentalism, Wooden pulled Slaughter and replaced him with Doug McIntosh, and allowed McIntosh to finish the game. To exacerbate the agony, Wooden knew dozens of Slaughter's friends and relatives were in the stands, since they were playing where he had attended high school.

Wooden made many such decisions in his remarkable career, never confusing leadership with popularity. The coach also knew that respect must precede popularity in leadership, and his tough decision and politically incorrect manner was validated when he reached the locker room after the game and was met by Slaughter, who had been waiting for him: "Coach, before someone gets the wrong impression, I want you to know that I understand. You had to leave Doug in there because he played so well, and I didn't. I wanted to play in the worst way, but I do understand and if anyone says I was upset, it's not true. Disappointed, yes, but upset, no. And I was very happy for Doug."[4]

Politically incorrect leaders understand that when they make the right decision rather than the convenient decision, they win and so does the team. Wooden said at one time:

Fairness is giving all people the treatment they earn and deserve. It doesn't mean treating everyone alike. That's unfair, because everyone doesn't earn the same treatment. That's why I didn't treat all players alike. I didn't treat Walter Hazzard like I treated Gail Goodrich. I didn't treat Bill Walton like I treated Keith Wilkes. Contrary to what you might think, it enhanced teamwork, because almost every player I coached knew that he would be treated fairly, that he would be given exactly what he had earned and deserved. They worked harder as a result. It's true in sports and elsewhere in life [5]

Boy oh boy, if they'd stop suing the Boy Scouts and attacking nativity scenes long enough to read, this quote would keep the hemorrhaging hearts at the ACLU awake at night, because Wooden shined the light of truth and wisdom on the corruption of political correctness with his philosophy. This coach made tidal waves and earned 10 titles as a result.

3. When Vince Lombardi coached the Green Bay Packers he exuded political incorrectness. He was direct and demanding, honest, results-oriented, played to win, had a low threshold for idiots, and held others accountable. He earned respect, then popularity. Lombardi knew that holding people accountable didn't mean you had to demean or disrespect them. After catching Max McGee sneaking out for the third time Lombardi remarked to

the perpetrator: "Max, I said that will cost you $500 and if you go again, it'll cost you $1,000. Max, if you can find anything worth sneaking out for $1,000, hell, call me and I'll go with you."[6]

Balancing respect with directness to Paul Hornung before the 1959 season:

I know your reputation here. I've investigated you very carefully. You have done things you shouldn't have done. . . . I trust you. I just don't want you to let me down. If you do, it'll be your ass.[7]

When establishing expectations to the rookies, Lombardi balanced clarity, empathy, and directness:

Some of you boys are having problems picking up your assignments. It's a tough task. You got so many plays to learn, so many moves to learn. If you make a mistake, if you drop a pass or miss a block, anything like that, hell, forget it. If we had a defensive back here who felt bad every time he got beat on a pass pattern, he wouldn't be worth a damn. Take an education, but don't dwell on it. Don't let it affect your play. You will drop passes. You will make mistakes. But not very many if you want to play for the Green Bay Packers.[8]

Hard-Charging Strategies

To evaluate your level of politically incorrect leadership, answer the following:

1. Have you set a high standard of performance and behavioral expectations for yourself? If not, don't even think about trying to hold others accountable for their performance, because you cannot lead credibly when your personal bar is dropped lower than your drawers. You prove you're not a wimp or a hypocrite when you're willing to demand more from yourself than your people.

2. Do you have clear performance and behavioral expectations for your team? Do you hold one as sacred as the other? Are those standards high enough? If not, people will tend to live down to them. It's not your job to make people feel warm and fuzzy with a soft set of expectations. Your job is to stretch people, not to maintain them. If your expectations have become cloudy or conveniently forgotten, it's time to redefine them for your team. Until you do, holding them accountable for attaining them is unreasonable.

3. Are you committed to making the right decision—rather than the convenient decision—when holding others accountable for results? If not, you're a wimp. If you cannot detach yourself from tradition and sentimentalism, you betray the best interests of your team and the organization.

4. Do you balance confrontation with empathy? The sole objective of holding others accountable is to improve performance and help them to grow. It is not to demean, disrespect, or humiliate. If you don't grasp this you know nothing of leadership; you know only tyranny.

Trait Four: Politically Incorrect Leaders Keep People Out of a Gray Area.

When you work with or for a great leader, you never have to guess where you stand. Politically incorrect leaders give people the feedback they need to know how they're doing and what they must do to improve. While Chapter 4 will deal with five different types of feedback, here we'll cover four key elements of feedback necessary to develop your people:

1. Effective feedback happens quickly after the performance. Delayed consequences are not effective. If someone does a great job and you delay in letting them know, the recipient perceives your effort as an afterthought. In fact, getting there late with feedback is often worse than not getting there at all.

   Since behavioral science teaches that behaviors that get rewarded and reinforced get repeated, you must pay attention and let people know quickly when they are doing well. At the same time, you must confront people just as quickly when they veer onto the wrong path. Failure to confront a poor performance with prompt feedback, in effect, reinforces the behavior, and you're guaranteed to see more of it. To pull off the delivery of fast feedback you'll need to spend more time off your slumbering behind and in the trenches of your business, observing and analyzing what's really going on. If you have more calluses on your rear end than on your feet you'll never give feedback fast enough to improve behavior.

2. Effective feedback is consistent. Feedback is most helpful when delivered consistently, not just at monthly or

annual reviews. Consistent feedback provides the necessary number of reinforcers required to create or improve habits and behavior.

3. Effective feedback is brutally honest. You need to be more like Dr. Phil than Dr. Feelgood. If your feedback fails to tell it like it is you will not impact the employee. In fact, you will tacitly encourage denial and delusion, and make it more difficult for them to change their behavior in the future. Being brutally honest doesn't mean you shout, demean, or disrespect. It simply means that you state the facts as you see them, without the sellout of rationalization or compromise. The difference between directness and cruelty is courtesy. Be respectful but firm.

4. Effective feedback is specific. Telling someone, "You had a great month" is a good start, but if you want to impact the employee and accelerate his or her development, point out precise areas that were executed well: "Jan, you were very tenacious with your follow-up calls last month, and it really made a difference in your results." Specificity also tells the employee you care enough to pay close attention to what he or she is doing. Being specific when offering feedback to turn around a poor performance is just as important as specificity when you reinforce the productive results of someone doing the job well.

The most effective feedback is face-to-face. You cannot effectively develop people via memo, e-mail, or voice mail. Again, this means you'll need to stay engaged with the people-work part of your job and not become so dazed by data and numbed by numbers that you descend from leader to analyst. You may recall that during the Iran hostage crisis, this style was the Jimmy Carter Rose Garden recipe for leadership irrelevance that helped cost him the election.

Politically Incorrect Leadership Traits Summary

During a radio interview I was asked who my favorite leaders of all time were in a number of areas: sports, military, business, politics, and overall. Obviously, there are no right or wrong answers to this question. We all have favorites, and my guess is that when you recall yours, you'll see they have many or all of the four traits listed in this chapter. It's probably safe to say that the leaders you admire most didn't run around all day trying to make sure everyone was happy. I'd also bet they held followers accountable, were honest and direct in their approach, and had high standards.

I've already shared some of the same leaders with you as I did with my interviewer. I told her the leaders I admired most in the given categories were Green Bay Packer head coach Vince Lombardi for sports; General George S. Patton for military; Jack Welch for business; Abraham Lincoln for politics; and Jesus, overall. All five of these men had all four of the politically incorrect traits listed in this chapter: They all gave their best to the best; were unconventional in their approach; held others accountable for results; gave brutally honest feedback, and had high standards they stretched others toward. They weren't nearly as interested in popularity and harmony as they were in results.

As important as political incorrectness was to each of these men, it is even more important for you today. You lead in more challenging times than they did. Change happens much faster today, and the people you lead are more complex: They are more highly educated, more diverse, more demanding, and more entitled than at any time in history. Thus, if you don't tighten up, toughen up, and adapt your leadership style to address the hand you've been dealt, you'll get run over and rendered irrelevant as a leader. This is your wake-up call. Either step up and respond or step aside and let a real leader take charge. The shelf life for wimpy leaders is becoming increasingly and mercifully brief.

Hard-Charging Strategies

To develop and apply the traits in this section you must:

1. Keep people out of a gray area. Otherwise, you betray them. If your people are great tell them they're great! And if they're failing, tell them that as well—then help them devise a plan to turn things around.

2. Don't worry about demotivating people by telling them bad news. You demotivate them more by keeping them guessing because you won't tell them how they're doing. Disappointment is always easier to handle than anxiety.

3. Engage your people with robust dialogue. Care enough to confront them when they're off-track and applaud

them and share their victories when they do well. Feedback is the breakfast of champions. Current champions and potential champions need it to pursue their potential. If you're too indolent or indifferent to give fast, honest, and consistent feedback to your employees then I have some feedback for you: Resign before you're fired. It will look better on your resume.

CHAPTER

2

Eliminate Entitlements: Send the Moochers Packing!

Peering into the PC Cesspool

The *Oakland Tribune* reported that police were forced to stop putting up DUI checkpoints in certain parts of the Bay area because activists complained they were catching too many illegal immigrants. When stopped at a checkpoint, drivers are required to show their driver's license and proof of insurance; as a result, dozens of lawbreaking sneaks had been snagged, creating an uproar from entitled immigrant advocates who say that it is unfair to lawfully catch unlawful inhabitants through lawful means. Go figure.

Business Lesson: When lawbreakers—or rule breakers—are given preference over the upright in your workplace, morale suffers and momentum slows. Good people first become enraged and then indifferent. Until you stop coming to the defense of those who mock your standards and hijack your credibility you will sabotage your team and pervert your culture. And whether you realize it or not, you do come to the aid of these people every time you pretend their poor performance isn't happening and fail to hold them accountable; each time you fail to give them honest feedback or impose consequences, or provide special perks and favors to help them get through the tough times—even when they don't deserve it. This tolerance is especially costly when it comes at the expense of productive people.

Leverage your strengths and weed out your weaknesses.

Otherwise, the best either leave or plateau, and the rest become hopelessly entitled and incorrigible, a.k.a. worthless.

Entitlements Have Run Amok

Politically correct leaders believe they have to be everything to everyone. Worse, they spend 80 percent of their time with the bottom 20 percent of performers, in an effort to elevate the miserable to mediocre. The penalty for this misuse of time and resources is severe, because while you coddle, hug, and burp the poor performers, your neglected top performers become indifferent and stagnate. Unfortunately, many business leaders have followed society's trend to weaken the strong in order to strengthen the weak. But business leadership requires brave hearts—not bleeding hearts. Sadly, leaders in both politics and business have betrayed productive citizens and workers in this regard.

Following is a brief background of entitlements gone nuts in society: a brief study of the decline of California. Pay close attention. While California is the whipping boy in this example, don't miss the fact that the same fate that befell the Golden State may await your enterprise—unless you collapse your welfare state and send the moochers packing.

The State of California: Poster Child for Entitlement

The State of California, un-affectionately referred to by its oppressed residents as the People's Republic of California, has the fifth-largest economy in the world. It also reached a budget deficit greater than the other forty-nine states combined: nearly $40 billion as recently as 2003!

With vast economic horsepower and the enormous revenue infusion to the state coffers of a 9 percent state income tax, how do you run up the mother of all deficits? Answer: Out of control entitlements to the uninvited and undeserving, for starters. Quite frankly, California has become the ultimate welfare state: A beacon of abundance for the homeless, unemployed, and uninvited illegal immigrants.

In the name of compassion—and political correctness—leftist California legislators have overtaxed the productive citizens and then entitled millions of moochers, turning the doers into donors to enrich lazy moaners. While we all have equal value as human beings, and are mandated by every major religion as well as plain old common sense to care for one another, a civilized society cannot survive if it condones, justifies, or rationalizes the breaking of laws because it deems the perpetrators are underprivileged.

Once you've read and digested the background on the illegal immigrant crisis and the ensuing examples of California entitlements gone berserk, you should consider any disgust you feel as a call to arms, and eliminate similar freebies in your own business before you ride the California recipe from pinnacle to pathetic.

Background: The Illegal Immigration Invasion— Assault by the Uninvited and Unwanted

Most Americans are woefully ignorant of the illegal immigrant crisis in our country. Those who attack our impotent immigration laws and the influx of the uninvited and unwanted are characterized as backward bigots. Let's look at the facts, and then you be the judge as to whether the crisis and the ensuing entitlements are truly lethal or just another "vast, right-wing conspiracy" to boot foreign objects from our shores. After you read each point consider the Business Lesson, which relates how the influence of society's weak-as-a-wet-bee thinking diminishes your business thinking. Then get serious and begin to leverage your politically incorrect leadership style to ward off the poison of entitlements and to send the freeloaders in your own organization packing.

The following facts are taken from studies done by the National Academy of Sciences.

1. There are currently an estimated 13 million illegal immigrants in the United States. Yikes! Just let that number sink in for a second. During World War II America had 10 million troops under arms. Today, an army of far greater numbers is within our borders, breaking our laws, cheating the system, and depleting our resources.

Business Lesson: Chances are good that you have a growing number of moocher employees who are depleting your resources as well. In fact, one of your chief concerns should be the high number of unemployed people on your payroll. Oh, they show up every day. They've just retired on the job. In fact, when they officially retire it will be for the second time. Don't pretend that it isn't happening. Face reality about your people, and force this same brutal realism between the ears of every manager cashing your paychecks. Take the kid gloves off and transform your welfare state into a meritocracy where people get what they earn and deserve and are not subsidized by the productive people in your business.

2. Illegal immigrants are just that: illegal. You can use politically correct terms like "undocumented worker" to try and soften the impact of their deeds, but the fact is that these people broke our laws to get here. Read my lips: Illegal immigrants are criminals. Think that's too harsh? Then look up the word "criminal" in the dictionary: a person who commits a crime. There's no gray area here. To reward criminals with amnesty or other considerations is to invite more of the same. The last time a blanket amnesty was offered to illegals, in 1986, 2.7 million took advantage of the citizenship offer.[1] Yet that same year the nation saw a dramatic increase in both illegal immigration and chain migration, wherein the newly minted "citizens" sponsored family members to come to the United States, proving again that if you build it—a welfare state—they will come. Both results ran counter to the reduction in immigration that lawmakers and their "let's share the love" lullabies assured us would occur. Representative Tom Tancredo (R-CO) put it well when he said we should dedicate more energy to enforcing existing immigration laws and less on finding ways to allow millions to skirt them. Note: In 1993 some of the recipients from the 1986 blanket amnesty were involved in the first World Trade Center bombing. Lesson: Don't trivialize the devastating impact of entitlements to the underdeserving. They are serious business for society and enterprise.

Business Lesson: When laws are allowed to be broken en masse, rules and standards for all institutions are diminished, as people begin to become desensitized to right and wrong and think anything goes, as long as they get away with their illicit behavior. When this thinking pervades your business, employees can rationalize everything from taking office supplies home for personal use—after all, you "owe" them—to coming in late to work, to web surfing for hours each week on your nickel. You either have standards or you don't. You either stand for something specific or fall for everything in general. Some leadership clowns afflicted with momma's boy meekness never figure this one out.

Hard-Charging Strategies

The major problems we face in society and in business didn't emerge overnight. They crept up steadily upon us over time, to reach disastrous proportions, and they are impossible to correct without an assault of major financial and human resources. Thus, you must:

1. Reject a too-tolerant mindset that causes you to depart from sound performance disciplines.
2. Make the right decisions rather than the convenient, easy, cheap, or popular decisions.
3. Sweat the small stuff in key areas of discipline. These areas have the potential to debilitate your corporate culture, misuse resources, loosen accountability, and estab-

lish a corrupt benchmark for performance that, when left unchecked, portend certain disaster.

4. Confront performance problems quickly. As the old saw goes, "shovel the piles while they're small." Whether in society or business, the discipline of meeting these matters head on, in their infancy, preserves cultural excellence and standards. Failure to do so invites decline. It really is that black and white.

Entitlement Example #1: The Impact of Illegal Immigration on California

With the background on the impact of illegal immigrants now in perspective, let's take a closer look and discover the contribution pandering to and entitling these illegal immigrants has levied upon the California budget crisis, and as we do, you can contemplate the costs incurred to your business when you unwittingly pimp to the wrong element among your workforce. The parallels are undeniable.

1. Of the estimated 13 million-plus illegal immigrants estimated to be in the United States, over one third is estimated to reside in California! This is why we're putting our focus on California as the epitome of a poorly run enterprise: stupidity, political correctness, and entitlements have reached critical mass in California: What it needs is an infusion of merit-based thinking and an expulsion of its pro-welfare tendencies. Your business may need the same.

Business Lesson: Remember, trends in business follow trends in society, so the same remedies and lessons can be applied to your own enterprise. Ignorance may be bliss, but if you ignore the connection here between society and business trends ignorance becomes very expensive bliss!

2. The aforementioned study by the National Academy of Sciences showed that the average illegal immigrant household represented a net fiscal drain on California of $3,500 per year. The *National Review* cited a report that estimates that each illegal immigrant in California will take $50,000 more from the state in services than he or she will contribute in taxes during his or her lifetime.[2] When you factor in the millions of illegals in California, you can quickly discern their contribution to the state's financial collapse.

Business Lesson: How many of your employees inflict a negative value on your organization, and how much longer will you coddle them? Be warned, today's PC mantra of tolerance will cause you to endure the shameless plunder of your resources to the brink of ruin—or beyond.

3. After capture, federal authorities buy illegal aliens a bus ticket to the city they were destined for, so they can show up at a court hearing—at which they rarely appear. Your tax dollars pay for this literal free ride. Here's a thought: When captured for breaking our laws, why not book these people, process them, delouse them, put them in an orange jumpsuit, lock them up in chains and

shackles, and transport them on a prison bus under armed escort to a court hearing? The reason this doesn't happen is simple: The ACLU would fill the court with hysterical lawsuits indicting law enforcement agencies for treating foreign lawbreakers *equally* with our home-grown criminals.

Business Lesson: That's precisely the problem with PC; poor performers and malcontents are actually treated *better* than other people! Think it's not true? With whom do you spend the most time and energy in your organization—the people on the bottom or the top people? Most likely, the bottom feeders—and when you do, you're telling your star performers this: "When you get really good and create great value for the organization, what you can expect in return is less time, attention, and resources from me." Wrong message! Another example of giving the wrong people preferential treatment is that the children of illegal immigrants pay in-state tuition charges at California universities, saving them thousands of dollars every year. This means that law-abiding, non-California residents and citizens of the United States—like many of you reading this book—sending their child to UCLA will pay twice the tuition than the children of illegal immigrant lawbreakers! How is this fair? Your good employees may be asking the same question. Examine where you invest your time and resources and ensure that poor performers are not being treated equally—much less better—than the productive employees in your business.

4. Our government is seriously considering allowing Mexicans working illegally within the United States

(lawbreakers) to collect Social Security benefits. According to press reports, we are close to adding Mexico to a list of 20 other countries currently participating in "totalization" agreements that allow workers who return to their nation of origin to collect Social Security payments. With identify theft and the pervasive corruption in Mexico, the potential for fraud and abuse is staggering. Think about this nonsense: There won't be enough Social Security dollars to fund your own retirement because the system is going broke, but let's make sure we take care of the lawbreakers and send them our money to boost their economy at the expense of law-abiding citizens.

Business Lesson: Before you get too indignant with this example of entitling the wrong element, consider if you might be a hypocrite. As suggested in the prior point, do you spend so much time, energy, and resources trying to elevate the miserable up to mediocre that you have nothing left to pour into your best people in the form of greater rewards, opportunities, and perks? If so, you're more of a caseworker than a leader. There's only so much to go around, and if too much is going to the undeserving you effectively turn your best performers into second-class citizens.

5. Half of all welfare usage in California is from immigrant households, and 32 percent of all illegal immigrant households receive benefits from at least one welfare program. Please read that last part again: Thirty-two percent of all illegal immigrant households (criminals) benefit from at least one welfare program. In addition

to welfare, illegal immigrants receive free emergency health care. They just have to show up at the hospital emergency room with a headache or stubbed toe and presto—we pick up the tab and their healthcare is "on the house." No wonder these people go to any extreme to get here and milk the mother cow. As a small business owner paying $1,503 per month for health insurance that covers only my wife, daughter, and me, I can't help wonder how much of this monthly premium goes to subsidize free healthcare for these lawbreakers.

Business Lesson: Based on these facts, here's a question for you to ponder: How many of your undeserving employees are plugged into your corporate dole roll? My guess is that it's more than you can afford to continue carrying. Think about the crazy logic of keeping these parasite employees: "Well, let's see here. . . . This person turns out below-average results, lowers morale, breaks momentum, and diminishes my personal credibility, so I wonder what I should do with him. . . . I've got it! I'll plug him into financial life support so he can hang around and continue to drain my business!" It's really not very funny, because what sounds insane has become all too common.

6. About half of all immigrants are too poor to pay income taxes. Yet, 50 percent of all kids in the California public school system are from immigrant families—a dramatic increase in the number of kids in schools without a corresponding increase in the tax base. American moms and dads, many working two jobs, are breaking their backs to pay enough taxes to fund the enlightenment of

outlanders. The proportion of this financial shakedown is obscene, and makes the IRS look like Salvation Army bellringers by comparison.

Business Lesson: This is precisely how your good performers feel when they are burdened by those who can't or won't do their share. When your productive employees must carry their load and the slackers' load they eventually compromise their own performance. The best way you can deliver to your fruitful people is to unburden them from having to carry the morons, misfits, and moochers corrupting your workplace who don't do their share, can't hit their goals, or won't live your values.

7. Former—recalled by fed-up citizens—California Governor Gray Davis had approved issuing illegal immigrants driver's licenses. This dangerous effort to further entitle and legitimize criminals was reversed by Governor Arnold Schwarzenegger.

Business Lesson: In your business you entitle and legitimize your own version of "illegals" every time you don't hold them accountable; when you fail to impose consequences for derelict performance, and worse of all, when you actually reward them for their poor work with more of your time and resources because they're "disadvantaged." Rather than give them a driver's license, you give them a license to fleece your corporate coffers and culture.

8. In an egregious attempt to buy support from the illegal constituency, fifth-column factions of the California legislature initiated lobbying efforts to gain illegal im-

migrants the right to vote. In this manner, they could become more powerful and elect candidates who promised further handouts and privileges.

Business Lesson: Don't miss the message here, because this is how entitlement works: Once you get a few crumbs you don't stop until you have the whole pie—or in this case, the whole country. Or in your organization's case, until the laggards infest and pillage your entire business.

The progression of freebies listed: welfare checks, free bus tickets, free education, free emergency medical care, the right to have a driver's license, and the current mandate to vote is exactly how entitlement works in society and in business: Once you start to give someone something for nothing there is no stopping the demands of scroungers. As abusive welfare programs have proven in the past: When you give someone something for nothing long enough, you make him or her good for nothing!

The same holds true for corporate benevolence systems that pander to and ceremoniously shower nonperformers with everything from automatic end-of-the-year raises, promotions based on tenure, Thanksgiving turkeys, donuts every Friday, and various other benefits in the name of "fairness and compassion" that are taken for granted and lose their positive effect, since people have come to believe they are owed them rather than have to actually earn them. An old saying goes: Give a man a fish and you feed him for a day. Teach him how to fish and you feed him for a lifetime. In today's PC society cadgers don't want to learn to fish. They've regressed from wanting something for nothing to demanding it, and have proven beyond doubt that when you give a man a fish you may feed him for a day, but when you give him another fish you start to make him good for nothing, because tomorrow he is no longer happy with a fish: He wants steak and lobster and wants it for free.

Entitlement Example #2: How the People's Republic of California Entitles the Homeless

California's benevolent, politically correct insanity doesn't stop with its infatuation with and the lavishing of perks on lawbreakers. They extend to the homeless, drunks, vagrants, and junkies.

Without a doubt, nonprofit organizations like the Salvation Army are the most effective and compassionate vehicles for dealing with society's needy. But the far-left freak show running San Francisco thought they had a better idea. Thus they gave panhandlers financial incentives to continue being bums, certificates they could exchange for food, and lo and behold, were amazed to discover that it increased panhandling and homelessness!

According to Lloyd Billingsly, editorial director of the Pacific Research Institute in San Francisco, "San Francisco's policy has been to give the homeless generous cash grants of up to $395 monthly, with few questions asked. The easy cash attracted what an Australian paper, unconstrained by Bay area political correctness, called a 'hobo boom'—a tide of vagrants, drunks, and junkies. The lesson here is that, as the movie *Field of Dreams* put it, if you build it, they will come. But they won't clean up after themselves." It's hard to feel good about how these people spend their monthly stipend as you see them publicly smoke, drink, and do drugs.

55

Locals and tourists alike will testify, as entitlements to this "body odor" brood increased so did their boldness and belligerence, turning one of the world's most beautiful cities into an international safe house for society's slouches. What could be more repulsive to a productive resident of San Francisco, burdened under an oppressive tax structure and imperious cost of living, than to walk to work and see, hear, and smell entitled freeloaders propped up against a wall, fly open, turning the city into their personal urinal—all done while on the way to pick up their $395 check for doing absolutely nothing but drain value from society? How about at least having these folks turn in a hefty bag of aluminum cans in order to collect their check? It might even make them feel better about getting their handout.

Business Lesson: If you don't make some waves and begin to redistribute time, energy, resources, and rewards according to what people earn rather than what they need you'll breed your own brand of bums. They may use indoor restrooms, but they're no less dangerous to morale and momentum.

Entitlement Example #3: Weakening the Strong to Strengthen the Weak

In life as in business, when the strong are weakened in order to strengthen the weak, the strong do reach a point when enough is enough, and leave the madness for saner ground.

According to the California State Board of Equalization about 80 percent of the state's revenue losses are a result of disappearing millionaires. The antibusiness bureaucrats in the state government have made it clear through high taxes, oppressive regulations, and liberal giveaways that they despise rich people, so the rich have retaliated by leaving.

The number of reported millionaires in California plunged by 15,000 in one two-year period, taking their jobs, talents, spending power, and tax base with them, proving the lesson that when the bar is set high the winners will love it and the losers will leave it—but when the bar is set low, the losers will love it and the winners will leave it.[3]

Business Lesson: Let me suggest how the winners in your organization leave the bar when it's too low. Sometimes they leave physically, but oftentimes they do so mentally and emotionally, by losing heart and one day ceasing to give the extra effort, losing their passion, and becoming discouraged, indifferent, and disgusted by the inequities your welfare state provides for less worthy performers.

Is Your Business on the Road to Becoming a California?

Before you get too sanctimonious and decry the madness in the Golden State, take a look at your own business and your personal leadership tendencies, revisit the Business Lessons included at the conclusion of each of the prior points, and answer the following questions as you search for entitlement and political correctness gone awry in your own back yard:

1. Are your performance and behavioral expectations high enough to stretch people, or are they set so low that people routinely hit them with little extra effort? Do

57

you set expectations so low that people live down to them? If you don't have the guts to set the bar high and equip people to reach them you are wasting everyone's time and simply taking up space at work. Since you can't or won't lead, you'd be better off to go find something you're good at.

2. Do your bonus and pay structures reward average or be-low performances? Can someone doing mediocre work still make a decent living, because your pay plan is so laced with entitlements that you are unconsciously re-warding, endorsing, and reinforcing substandard re-sults, and thus encouraging more of the same? If you can afford to throw money away on moochers you have too much of it and deserve to lose it. Keep on rewarding incompetents and eventually you'll become just like them.

3. Are people held accountable for outcomes? Are you a maniac for results, or do you continually rationalize shortfalls because the person put forth a valiant effort? Are there consequences for failing to get the job done? If the only consequence you impose is another hot-air speech about how things had better improve I can promise you that your people mock you behind your back. You're a laughingstock and you're the only one who hasn't figured it out.

4. Do you have minimum performance standards in each quantifiable position, so that employees failing to attain acceptable levels basically fire themselves? Or do you appoint yourself public defender for the lazy, the lousy, and the lost, giving them six second chances to inflict

themselves on your culture? If so, be thankful there is no prison for poor leaders because you'd be on death row.

5. Is the best person for the job promoted or do you reward tenure, diversity, or genetics over results? If you promote for reasons other than outright merit you're betraying your most able people and the company overall. In fact, your weaker-than-worm-whiz leadership style is an embarrassment: Pack up quietly and leave after you close today. On second thought, go ahead and leave right now. No one will even notice.

6. Do you have long-term employees you classify as "loyal" even though they haven't produced results since Moby Dick was a minnow? Don't confuse loyalty with tenure, because tenure can become a license for laziness. Shouldn't true loyalty be defined as "performance"—whether someone has worked for you 10 days or 10 years? If you measure loyalty by the number of years someone puts into your company, go get the biggest dictionary you can find and look up the word "loyal" and you'll notice that nothing concerning a length of time is mentioned. In case you missed it the first time: Loyalty is performance. If you have an employee that has both longevity and performs well you have the ultimate employee. But if you must choose between the two, pick performance!

7. Do you pay your top people substantially more and give them unequal amounts of opportunities and resources, or do you endeavor to allocate your resources communally across the board? Are you afraid to shower perks, favors, and rewards on the top performers who have

earned them, because you might offend the wannabes, wieners, and whiners in your ranks? Sometimes the folks at the bottom need to be jolted; you need to get their attention, and you must send them the right message. When you give your best to the best and less to the rest, the rest will get motivated and try to become like the best—or they will get demoralized and leave. Either way, life gets good!

8. Where do you invest most of your time and energy: with the miserable, trying to elevate them to mediocrity, or with your great players—with the intent of making them greater yet? Most leaders work with weaklings because they're easier. They don't talk back. They're impressed with your title. They're scared and will listen to what you say. The top people aren't as impressed with you; they may know more than you and are more independent and aggressive. If you shun your top people for these reasons your leadership is both cowardly and caustic. If you haven't yet taken the advice I offered at the end of point five earlier, it's time to get moving!

9. Do you give out Christmas bonuses because it's Christmastime or because people have actually earned them? Have they become an entitlement that people expect to receive regardless of their performance? If you're foolish enough to throw money away because of ceremony and sentimentalism then go for it. When entitlements become expected, with no merit basis, they are never appreciated; never enough and never ending. Eliminate all Christmas bonuses that aren't connected to performance measurements. They're just a more compassion-

ate form of welfare that people come to expect each December just because they show up, and not because their results warranted the reward.

10. Do you dish out end-of-the-year raises because it's the end of the year or because people went the second mile? Have raises become automatic—based on tradition rather than outcomes? The next time a moocher asks for a raise, tell him or her that your new raise policy is to reward results rather than requests and then have them put in writing what they've done over and above their normal work duties to earn the raise. You'll never hear from them again.

11. Do you have people working for you who are far more focused on what they are owed than what they owe? Do they routinely put in a minimum of effort and expect a maximum return? Do they do just enough to get by, or do they do what is required and then some? You can't build an elite company with "just enough" people. You need to do just enough to get them out the door and get some real help. Elite companies are built by second-milers, not by losers who limp and barely make it through the first 100 yards.

12. Do you consistently put the good of the team ahead of the good of any one individual? Or do you make exceptions to rationalize, trivialize, and marginalize, retaining your shirkers? The good of the team must come first and that means it comes before your own needs and convenience as a leader as well. If you can't subordinate your own welfare and ego for the good of the team then I'd like to express my sincerest sympathies for the

people suffering under your selfish, sadistic leadership. If they ever decide to revolt against you, I'd write the first check to support their cause.

Environment Dictates Behavior

One doesn't have to look far to validate the principle that environment dictates behavior. Because of the too-tolerant and entitled culture that has developed in California during recent years, illegal aliens and homeless bums flock to the state while millionaires flee it. The support and edification of society's wrong elements have created culture-rot.

Environment dictates behavior in your business as well. This is why in the prior chapter I outlined four politically incorrect traits you must adopt to help you create a performance-based culture. One of the biggest wastes of time leaders engage in is to try to change the behavior of their employees without first changing the workplace environment. As a result, behavior might change for an hour, a day, or a week at most, but soon returns to its prior state—because the environment in which the behaviors were taking place remained static.

The key to changing your environment is to change your own leadership style as outlined in Chapter 1. Once you differentiate your people, innovate rather than optimize, give faster, honest, and consistent feedback, hold people accountable for results and begin seeking improvement over being approved, your culture will change. When your culture changes behavior will improve, and when behavior improves so will the results. This is not rocket science—but it does take plenty of tenacity and discipline. Tending to your environment takes constant attention. It's like a garden. You must weed and seed it often. Turn your head too long and the weeds will take the garden. Your own garden may be under siege as you read these words.

As a politically incorrect leader you must take personal responsibility for creating and sustaining a performance-based environment—a meritocracy—and not allow entitlements to drain the life from your enterprise. This is an awesome responsibility, and one you must confront with courage, or the day will come when no one takes you seriously as a leader. Whatever your workplace environment feels like on a day-to-day basis is a reflection of your leadership. This fact should either make you bloat with pride or shrink in shame. But this isn't about fault—it's about fixing it. So get off your behind and climb into the trenches and shape your environment, rather than let it shape you.

Hard-Charging Strategies

Whether in business or society, when expectations are too low there is no accountability for results, and mediocrity is tacitly endorsed with subsidies and entitlements—chaos ensues. Culture is weakened, productive behaviors are diminished, and positive outcomes plummet. In politically correct societies or businesses where anything goes and there are no winners or losers—just contenders—solid, sustainable success is an impossibility. Thus you must:

1. Set the bar high: Give people what they earn and deserve, nothing more and nothing less, and hold people

responsible for the results of their actions. Anything less provides a willing host for the soot of entitlement and its subsequent devastation.

2. You must assume the role as an environmental thermostat, not a thermometer. Thermostats are active and control the temperature of the environment, whereas thermometers are passive, reacting and responding to whatever happens to be going on.

3. Step up, create a meritocracy and chase corporate welfare and your homegrown disciples of entitlement out the door before it's too late. Entitlement doesn't make someone a bad person. But it does make them a bad fit for an organization aspiring to become elite.

4. Make some waves today, tomorrow, and from here on out to send the moochers packing before they fasten an anchor that sinks your career and drowns your organization in a politically correct, entitlement-based quagmire of manure. Don't think it can't happen to you because, in all likelihood, it already has. Just because you don't see it or don't want to see it doesn't mean you're not being bilked on the installment plan by the entitled, the "loyal," and the just plain lazy.

Don't Confuse the Scoreboard for the Game!

Peering into the PC Cesspool

The *New York Times* wanted to flaunt its diversity program to the world and trumpet a scoreboard that validated its long-time promotion of color, gender, and ethnicity over character and competence. For their poster child they chose Jayson Blair, who came to the *Times* on a minority recruiting program. Soon after he arrived, his supervisors noted that his game was sloppy and his integrity suspect: consistently high error rates and slack work habits. Before every Blair promotion designed to intensify the scoreboard's light of diversity, at least one editor had pointed out his deficient skills and blatant inaccuracies: The *Times* ran 50 corrections on Blair stories in just 42 months.[1]

Blair also exhibited serious character flaws by distributing confidential documents and boozing it up in bars on the *Times'* tab. Management-in-denial continued to promote Blair at breakneck speed, ignoring and sometimes suppressing reports of his professional inadequacy as well as his emergence as a pathological liar. In order to maintain the mirage of their politically correct, diversity-driven scoreboard, the *Times* ignored Blair's game and paid a just price in humiliation and lost credibility when Blair was caught in his plagiarism by the *San Antonio Express-News*.[2] Ironically, Blair had been forced to resign from the University of Maryland student newspaper for precisely the same treachery he perpetrated at the *Times*—proving once again that the greatest predictor of future performance is past performance.[3]

Business Lesson: The Jayson Blair debacle is a textbook example of how leaders who confuse the scoreboard for the game sow seeds of future fiascos and create short-term results built on a foundation of sand. By either ignoring the game altogether as long as the scoreboard is flashing the right result, or by not caring enough to look closely enough to see how the game is being played, you set yourself and your organization up for definitive and inevitable failure. In this case, the *Times* ran more than four full pages purporting to itemize and apologize for Blair's sleaziness, blaming the assailant even while they remained the enabler.

Was the *Times'* failure to confront and correct Blair a racial preference issue, a performance issue, or a little of both? You be the judge. But don't miss the message—and the inevitable consequences for confusing the scoreboard for the game in your own business.

Don't Get So Seduced By the Scoreboard That You Fail to Watch the Game

Many corporate execs today are like New Testament Pharisees. In the absence of substance they primp, position, and posture to create a mirage of legitimacy. The phonies at Enron, WorldCom, and Tyco are contemporary examples of holy-rolling rabble that lead by personal convenience rather than personal example, pimping out their values for valuables and temporarily lighting up the scoreboard while they bilked and pillaged the game. These lying, thieving punks in pinstripes hoodwinked the world, and are blatant proof that you cannot afford to become so obsessed with the end that

67

you ignore the means. In an age when perception trumps reality it's vital that you become more skeptical and dig beneath the facade of apparent results in your own organization, to more closely examine *how* they're being produced. Why should you be a bit paranoid? Because *how* you or your people are getting the results portends more about your future than the results themselves. Savvy leaders know the *how* is where they're headed. For instance, rather than stand back and champion a manager breaking new records or let your own pat on the back turn into a massage because of the results you're getting, make some waves and take an honest look at the *how* to more clearly determine the rightness or wrongness of your course:

1. Are you getting the job done on the backs of people, by pushing, abusing, and intimidating? Are you a micromanager, getting overinvolved with everyone and everything, committing the leadership sin of being too dependent upon yourself rather than building a team to help carry the load? If so, your success will be temporary, morale will diminish, and good people will leave.

You may recall that "Chainsaw" Al Dunlap embraced this abusive management style as he turned around failing companies and personally pocketed hundreds of millions of dollars, lighting up Wall Street's scoreboard and looking great for a while. But his derelict game plan made his success unsustainable. What went around came around when "Chainsaw" Al himself got the axe while at Sunbeam after his obnoxious style went too far and made him as welcome as a Kennedy at the Kopechne family reunion.

2. Are you getting the numbers because you work double shifts and never take a day off? If this is the case, you're headed for trouble because you will eventually burnout, plateau, and then plunge, taking your organization down the toilet with you. If you work long and hard but ultimately work dumb you'll eventually discover that you can't convert your work ethic or good intentions into sustainable results. But normally by the time you find out, and are found out, it is too late. Consider this a preemptive warning shot.

Former CEO and Aussie Jacques Nasser followed this path to demise at Ford as he lost focus on core products, alienated the dealer network, burned through billions in cash, and nearly bankrupted the company before being forced to resign. No one questioned his work ethic—it was his asininity that was overlooked for too long. It will take years for Ford to recover from the plunderer from Down Under.

3. Are you getting results because you've created a culture of discipline (a good thing) or because you are a tyrant who disciplines (a dangerous thing), imposing your will on the team through the sheer force of your personality? If it's the latter, you'll get an occasional fear-based adrenaline rush of temporary results that plummets faster than your willpower at a Krispy Kreme counter.

Jim Collins, in *Good To Great* (HarperCollins, 2001) tells how Stanley Gault, while head of Rubbermaid, built a company that fell apart after he left and wound up as acquisition fodder for Newell. Gault was a self-proclaimed tyrant that never built a team and failed to create a culture that could sustain longterm vitality after his departure.[4] Shamefully, he betrayed the interest of Rubbermaid employees and shareholders by subordinating their best interests to his own ego. This pharaoh marched his company to the banks of the Nile and smack into the guts of the gators.

4. Are you getting results because you're in the right place at the right time? This one may bruise your ego a bit, but don't go into denial if it is true. Do you have a product or service so hot it literally sells itself? Situations like these can make you lazy; before long you'll have an inflated sense of self-worth. All products are still subject to business cycles, and once the novelty wears off or the competition wakes up the dip in demand will expose the sins of the good times. Humble yourself, keep this in perspective, and maintain your daily disciplines. Enjoy the portion of your success that you've actually earned and that hasn't been gifted on you, but don't believe your own headlines. Chances are, you're not that good.

IBM had been the Big Daddy in computers and related services for so long their culture had become indifferent to customers, mired in complacency, and allergic to change. In other words, they had gotten lazy, arrogant, and stupid. Besieged by competitors and customer defections, IBM was in danger of collapse. When Lou Gerstner took the reins and turned around Big Black & Blue, he returned the company back to the tenets of basic execution, and instituted "Operation Bear Hug" to reconnect with customers. In this initiative, each of the top 50 people at IBM would personally visit five of IBM's biggest customers to find out firsthand what their needs and wants were.[5] This renewed focus on business basics, a genuine display of humility, and appropriate keister-kissing helped catapult IBM back to prominence.

5. Are market conditions so strong that you are "drafting" on the strength of economic helium? Don't mistake a bull market for brains! Remember the Internet boom and bust and all the business plans and entrepreneurs without products, profits, or prospects that were paper-millionaires one day and bankrupt the next! Hold you and your team strictly accountable for executing vital daily disciplines, especially when seductive economic conditions exist, and resist the temptation robust times present for cockiness, laziness, abandonment of sound business principles, making tough decisions and necessary changes. To put it another way: continue to fix your roof while the sun is shining. Don't wait for it to leak or collapse to grab your attention and return you back to solid business principles, humbled, broke, and embarrassed.

How many booms have you witnessed, in industries ranging from oil to real estate to banking to automotive retail sales to the airlines, where the leaders seemed to think the good times would last forever and they'd never see another poor day? These booms made the leaders look a lot smarter than they were. Buoyed by their apparent success, they abandoned viable business principles, took their employees and customers for granted, overextended their resources, and failed to renew themselves in the absence of crisis only to discover that they really weren't that smart after all. Surprise! The economy still travels in cycles, and when you forget, the penalties are harsh: pawning your Rolex, selling your second and third homes, putting your kids back in public schools, and protecting the assets you have left under a shield of bankruptcy. You can only pity the kin and bored-stiff friends of these financial has-beens, as they're obliged to indulge countless choruses of how rich life was back in the "good old days," and who must politely suffer blowhard tales about the big one that got away.

When the Game Is Solid

Finally, some good news. If you're getting results because you set clear and high expectations, give people the training and feedback they need to succeed, lead from the trenches of your business, treat people like assets rather than expenses, hold them accountable for outcomes, and as a result have built a solid team that sustains success and doesn't miss a beat when you're absent, you're a model leader, building long-term vitality for your organization—and you will reap a continual harvest of results. You should also recognize and reward this same ability in others, because people who can consistently develop other people to higher levels are rare and worth their weight in Krugerrands.

By following the examples of Dave Maxwell at Fannie Mae, who not only saved the company but left a leadership team in place that took it to even higher heights after his departure; to Jack Welch at GE or Jesus of Nazareth, you can build long-term success and ensure prosperity for your organization by building a bench of leaders to step up and carry the ball in your absence. And contrary to conventional wisdom, the truest measure of your leadership is not how well people perform while you're in the workplace nitpicking them, threatening them, and breathing down their necks. The truest measure of your leadership is how well they do when you aren't around; be it a day off, vacation, or retirement.

If you're one of countless bantamweight bosses who is afraid to be away from the office for a day to attend a meeting, a seminar, or just to take a day off, you have serious work to do, because the fact that your people are so dependent on you indicts your leadership rather than affirms it. Resist the temptation of the insecure, clueless leaders who are reluctant to delegate, push power down to others, or mentor high potentials because they think it will diminish their own effectiveness. The most effective leaders are astute and secure enough to realize there is no success without a successor. Only idiots believe they're indispensable. What de Gaulle said made sense: "The graveyard is filled with indispensable men."

"Just Win, Baby" Is a Recipe for Disaster

Unfortunately, in today's age of instant gratification and "just win, baby," you may be tempted to ignore the *how* as long as someone is producing the *what*. This philosophy is reckless. If you're just looking at the numbers you or others produce you're either lazy, irresponsible, or ignorant. You're not looking hard enough or far enough, because as important as the numbers are, they are lagging indicators of what has already occurred. They show up too late to detect and correct poor performance. It's fine to be a student of numbers, but more important to be a student of disciplines, behaviors, and culture, because that's exactly where your numbers are headed. This means you'll have to spend less time charting results and poring over reports while you collect calluses on your backside and more time charting the course, in the trenches getting calluses on your feet and hands as you more actively assess where your business is headed and work smarter to impact it. Since the front line determines the bottom line, you need to camp out there from time to time.

Evaluate your team often and determine how they're getting results, as well as how you personally get results. If you're bringing home the bacon by doing the right things, keep it up, and don't falter in your resolve. Likewise, if your people do the same, affirm and acclaim them.

The How Doesn't Apply Only to Leaders

While I've used leaders as examples in this chapter, you can use the same "how is where you're headed" strategy to evaluate the performance of salespeople or other nonmanagement personnel in your business:

1. Is a salesperson getting great numbers because he's a customer-hog and throws enough opportunities against the wall so that what sticks makes for a good month? If so, the moment customer traffic dies down or the other

salespeople have had enough and decide to freeze out this greedy schmuck, stick a fork in him, because he's done.

2. Does the person get great numbers because he lies to customers; saying anything necessary to make the sale, with the thought that he (or the manager) will fade the heat when it arises? Fortunately, this trend normally doesn't take much time to show up, unless you have a manager who turns a blind eye to this madness and sells out your standards in return for the numbers. If this is the case, fire the manager first; then the salesperson.

3. Does the salesperson put up great numbers because he lives at the business, working every available hour and all days off? This salesperson is headed for trouble at home with what is left of his family, or in the areas of physical or mental health. Either way, it's just a matter of time before this rising star becomes a meteor shower. Teach him to work smarter so he can spend less time at work and actually have a life. If employees aren't any good at home they won't be any good at work either— at least not for long, because they'll be lugging the home front's baggage into the workplace, creating distractions and diluting their focus.

If any of the above describes the *how* concerning your people, you are in for a roller-coaster ride with employees who will never achieve consistently spectacular results. On the other hand, if they're putting up great numbers because they are disciplined, self-motivated, and persistent, you should sit down with them and, together, wrack your brains to determine what more you can do as their leader to help them take their talents to an even higher level: what barriers can you remove, what discretion can you push down to them, and what logistical support can you provide. One of the best questions you can ask one of these employees is simply, "What do you need from me in order to become even more successful?" And then follow through and deliver it quickly.

Do You Have a "Blair" in Your Lair?

While Jayson Blair is a certified liar and cheat, he is certainly not alone in his field or outside it. *USA Today*'s Jack Kelley was also putting up a fat scoreboard. While Blair was a rising star, Kelley was established as the Big Dipper. For a while, both scoreboards screamed, "We've hit the big time!" but clear eyes eventually noticed their sleazy game and peeked under the covers of their performance, much to the humiliation of both papers and reporters. Both men plagiarized for pleasure and lied for sport as they violated the trust of their companies and readers. In each case it is now well established that some of their bosses suspected trouble long before they confronted the issue (that darned politically correct reluctance to offend strikes again), opting for harmony over truth and learning the hard way that when you ignore defective performance or values or fail to face reality concerning your people, you unwittingly become a collaborator in the havoc they inflict. If you take nothing else of value away from this chapter, this one point alone will make it worth the read.

Now, before you shake your sanctimonious head in disgust or wag your finger in judgment, take a good look at your own current or potential Blairs and Kelleys. Read between the lines of their results, becoming a student of discipline, behaviors, and cultures, and keep the following at the forefront of your mind as you do: We live in undisciplined times. Morons from all walks want the prize without paying the price. If they spent as much time developing discipline (the *how*) as they did looking for shortcuts to the *what*, they could all retire to Malibu. But since this isn't the case, you'll have to establish that the "just get the numbers at any cost" mentality is a death sentence for your business, and instead create a culture of discipline to do the right things day in and day out.

To pull this off you'll need disciplined people, disciplined thought, and disciplined execution. In other words, you need employees who are ready, willing, and able to work within the disciplines of the priorities you establish and take action on them consistently. This doesn't require genius but it does take loads of commitment. It constitutes a *how* that transforms your business into a rocket ship, leaving the roller coaster for those politically correct, "hear no evil, see no evil" fools opting to sell out their standards and values in exchange for immediate results—even though doing so ensures inevitable derailment.

Hard-Charging Strategies

1. Analyze your employees' and your own performance and honestly determine how they and you are getting results. If your scoreboard presently looks good, but the game you're playing is built on a house of cards, change the plays now before it is too late. You can't fool the scoreboard forever. You will reap what you sow; maybe

not overnight, but certainly over time. While you may "Blair" your way through for a while with smoke and mirrors, in the end reality manifests itself—in its most nasty and hideous manner. Don't kid yourself into believing you might be the exception. That kind of ignorance and arrogance guarantees your decline.

2. Beware of one-month wonders. The business world is filled with sparklers whose light shines brightly and briefly right before they plunge into obscurity. You must do better. Care enough about your people and organization to lift the veil of ostensible success and face reality about current efforts and strategies and where they're taking you. The politically correct response to great results is to unquestioningly nod, applaud, and not ask questions or "mess with your success." In fact, when business is going well the practice of digging deeper and examining the *how* will seem like an unnatural act. After all, why make waves? If it ain't broke, don't fix it, right? Wrong! If you don't make waves you'll drown; if you don't mess with your success a competitor will, and if it's not broke then break it and make it better, before yesterday's peacock becomes tomorrow's feather duster.

The Power of Profiling

Don't be alarmed by the term "profiling." I'm not talking about the taboo, politically incorrect practice that effectively identifies criminals and terrorists and preempts their attack. Instead, I'm promoting business profiling, in order to counter and remedy the loosey-goosey behaviors and failed accountability that permitted the corrupt results identified in this chapter by the likes of Blair, Kelley, or your own version of these men.

Since human beings reach their potential in structured environments, you need a specific plan to grow you, your employees, and your organization, because you can rest assured that you will not wind up at a higher performance level by accident, and neither will your people. It takes deliberate thought and action. You may have a fairly clear idea of the heights you'd like to reach—the scoreboard—but you are in danger of failing miserably if you don't give enough forethought to how you'll get there—the game plan.

If you don't think deeply about your business and profile the next performance level you aspire to reach you'll operate out of instinct, shoot from the hip, and make it up as you go along. Profiling is hard work, and if you're a typical by-the-seat-of-the-pants leader you may work long and hard in your business but probably don't take enough time to step back and work *on* your business. You may not be facing reality about your people, strategy, or general direction. And if you misdiagnose what is holding you back from reaching your goals, you will prescribe the wrong solution and never build the sustainable success you want and think you deserve.

In addition to deliberately profiling your next desired business level of performance, you should also profile and create a deliberate plan to grow and develop your highest potential people. In fact, failing to deliberately plan and mentor their progress allows undesirable and destructive employee behaviors to evolve, which creates the next Blair or

Kelley in your organization. You can also use this profiling technique to fuel and direct your own growth.

Profiling causes you to do the following three tasks:

1. Determine exactly where you are in key performance metrics, rather than rely on your gut. Frankly, until you face reality about where you really are—your last 90-day average, not selectively remembering that record quarter 2 years ago—you'll never credibly create your future. In fact, you'll do just as well going to a fortune-teller.

2. Determine exactly where the next performance level is for you, your organization, or your people. The key here is to be specific by using definite quantifiable measurements; not warm and fuzzy foolishness, like, "We aspire to be the best we can be."

3. Think specifically about what you will do to close the gap between your current status and your desired destination, by working through a series of questions that narrow your focus and cause you to get specific about getting better. Get a pen and paper and work through the following two exercises. They have the potential to radically change the course of your business and your team. If you choose to skip this now and read on, realize that the chances of your coming back to ever do this exercise are remote. Don't be lazy and don't be in a hurry. Get in a quiet place, eliminate all distractions, and take some time to proactively think about your business. Thinking is hard work, which is why so few people do it. I expect you to do better and be better than those sorry souls.

The Power of Profiling: Business Unit

We'll start with profiling the next performance level for the business unit you are most directly responsible for.

Evaluate where your key performance averages are over the past 90 days in the most vital metrics applicable to your business. Don't guess! Use real numbers if you want real results. These can include metrics ranging from staffing numbers, gross sales, unit sales, net profit, customer satisfaction scores, account receivables, and the like.

A. Profile the desired targets in each of these areas that you want to reach within the next 90 days. Again, no touchy-feely sound bites here: just quantifiable targets. If they're not measurable you're subconsciously planning to fail, since you're afraid to lay it on the line and claim a destination you'll know for certain whether you attain. Don't leave yourself loopholes. I don't want any jellyfish readers fouling up the strategies in this book because they don't have the guts to do them right. When you profile your desired targets you're entering the no-wimp zone. Now do it! Be specific!

B. List at least two strategies to address each of these objectives. Be as specific as possible. Remember Strategy 101: Effective strategies hit centers of gravity, high-leverage targets that bring forth substantial return. When you choose strategies think of yourself as a military commander preparing to overtake a country. Obviously you have many potential targets to bomb, but not all of them have equal value. Bombing an abandoned farmhouse won't bring you the same return as taking out a power station. Your job is to choose the highest-leverage targets possible and hit them simultaneously and in the shortest span of time. By executing this you overwhelm the current system and don't give the status quo a chance to bounce back and reestablish itself.

On the other hand, by adopting a style of tinkering, tampering, and tweaking, you'll never go far enough fast enough to put a dent in the status quo and create lasting change. In fact, this may shed light on why so many of your past change efforts never got out of the gates: They didn't go far enough, fast enough.

C. Describe how you will tactically implement these strategies. Again, be specific. Include when you will begin, whom you must get involved, and what your personal involvement will be. Keep in mind that the strategies are the *what* and the tactics are the *how*. The most brilliant plan is absolutely useless if you can't execute it. Frankly, this is where most leaders drop the ball. They just can't implement and execute the plan. Thus, they fail and are eventually fired. Good riddance.

D. Meet with your management team to clarify objectives, review and discuss your strategies and tactics, and to narrow priorities into a cohesive plan to reach in the next 90 days.

You may change the format of the business unit profiling technique to fit your organization's needs. This is an exercise you should perform often, reevaluating and adjusting your strategy, staying fresh and focused. By focusing on the profile—the game—you don't leave your ideal scoreboard to chance. Important reminder: While it's your privilege and responsibility to define direction, you're foolish not to involve others in devising the strategy and the implementation for bringing it about, because people will support what they help create but they must first weigh in before they buy in.

After you work through this exercise you will have a real chance of actually hitting your objectives, since you took the time to specifically identify them and put into place a high-impact, thoughtful strategy for success. Throughout implementing the strategy you must stay flexible. Lock like a laser on your objectives but don't fall in love with your plan. If you've given your plan a fair chance and are executing it well but it's still not bringing results, you're probably hitting the wrong target or the right target at the wrong time, and you'll need to change the plan. There's no shame in changing your plan. What's shameful and futile is sticking with a bad one.

Profile Your People

You can use the same profiling technique to deliberately develop your high-potential people. Too many leaders think that their people will grow as a natural consequence of showing up at work each day. This is a fantasy. Growth is not automatic; death is. Growth must be intentional. I don't care how much experience someone has, just because they show doesn't mean they grow. Fifteen years experience is worthless if the employee spent 15 years doing dumb things, the wrong thing, or next to nothing. It's also worthless if the person stopped learning anything after the first year and doesn't really have 15 years experience, but one year repeated over and over 15 times! To effectively develop your people you must customize a plan to fit the person as a unique individual. Decide who on your team has the highest upward mobility: the ready, willing, and able. They must be three for three. Many people are ready and willing to grow but are not able. They don't have the capacity for any more than they are carrying, and oftentimes their ambition exceeds their competence, such as Senator John Edwards and his now infamous and laughable boast: "I'll beat George Bush in his own backyard." A very ambitious remark that was hindered by incompetence and wishful thinking. Bigmouths that don't have the competence to walk their talk are the canker sores of your organization, as they annoy, irritate, and distract your most competent workers.

On the other hand, some who are able are not willing to grow. Early in my management career I was incredibly naive, a.k.a. ignorant. I thought that everyone wanted to improve; that everyone wanted to grow, that everyone wanted to reach their fullest potential as a human being. In retrospect, as I reflect on thoughts like these I'm convinced someone must have slipped some LSD into my Diet Coke. Hard truth: This planet is littered with lackeys who treat life like a dress rehearsal, and are quite content to be stuck in a rut as long as it means they don't have to learn anything new, break a sweat, take responsibility, or actually change something in their miserable existence they call a life. These people constipate the free enterprise system. They die at forty and aren't buried until they're eighty, all the while not understanding the fuss about reaching their potential. This doesn't mean they're bad people—it simply means they will add marginal value to your organization, and that you should limit the time and resources you invest in them.

With all you have on your plate, you really don't have the time to smack these idlers on the head with a bat and drag them around the bases.

Follow These Steps to Mentor and Develop Your Highest Potential People

The Power of Profiling: The Individual

To deliberately develop a high potential employee on your team you must do the following:

1. Write the name of this person in a notebook: Profile there what this person must do to reach the next performance level; the point where his or her improved abilities will make a marked difference in results. Be specific: Learn how to hold a meeting, conduct interviews, do the inventory, produce certain reports, improve attitude, and the like.

2. List next how you propose to close the gaps between where this person is and how he or she will reach the next performance level. This plan should include the following:

    A. What this person must *start* doing to close this gap: skills to improve, how they will be improved, and when.

    B. What this person must *stop* doing to close this gap:

    C. What this person must *do more of* to close this gap:

85

D. What this person must *do less of* to close this gap:

E. What your mentorship role will be in these areas to close this gap:

- List specific tasks you will perform with this person so they learn to do it:
- Broaden his or her discretion and decision-making latitude in these areas:
- Invest in training in these specific areas:
- Delegate the following tasks to this person:
- Give faster and more direct feedback to reinforce or redirect in these areas:

Again, customize this outline to best fit your leadership style and your people. The key is to get more intentional about growing a team; to do so by design, and not expect that a great team will evolve by accident or by luck.

Profiling individuals is a form of mentoring that has become a lost art in many businesses. Leaders move so fast today that they don't take the time to pour themselves into high potential people, and oftentimes have little more than incidental contact with them. I don't suggest that you attempt to mentor more than one or two people simultaneously, because if you do it right it will take a large time investment. But the payoff down the line is substantial, as you build a bench of more highly capable people who create a culture of sustainable success and long-term vitality in your business. Ideally, as you are mentoring someone using this profiling technique, your protégé will use the same profiling technique to mentor his or her own high-potential people. In this manner you are deliberately building leaders at all levels in your organization and creating a *how* that will continue to turn out consistent and world-class *whats*.

Mentoring is an ancient idea, but it may be brand-new to your organization. Socrates mentored Plato. Plato mentored Aristotle. Aristotle mentored Alexander the Great and Alexander the Great conquered most of the world. This stuff works, so get with it!

Hard-Charging Strategies

1. By first determining what the person must accomplish and then designing how to execute you have the game plan necessary to effectively lead people to a higher level, and to systematically build a team of people capable of contributing at higher performance levels. When I was a young and dumb manager (the words young and dumb are often synonymous) I used to think that if a group of people showed up at the same time and same place for a certain number of weeks, months, or years a team would naturally develop. Wrong. Without a deliberate plan, oftentimes a band of mercenaries develops: A gang or mob appears. Great teams are built with strategic intent; you start the process by leveraging the abilities of your high-potential people using the profiling technique in this chapter. You can't afford to spend time and energy with everyone equally. Politically correct wimps use this socialistic brand of leadership and reap a banquet of mediocrity. You have an obligation to invest more time, energy, and resources into your best people. Failure to do this betrays your entire

organization. (At this point in the book, this should be crystal clear.)

2. Use your profiling plan as a coaching tool to offer feedback on the progress an employee is making, or to suggest new courses of direction when he or she falls off-track.

3. Throughout the mentoring process be cognizant of what you cannot teach others: You can't teach them attitude, character, talent, drive, or a high energy level. They must bring these traits to the table, because you can't put in what was left out—all you can do is draw out what was left in, and if they are deficient in these critical areas for success, it's time to move on and find someone that's giving you something to work with. Don't kid yourself and try to be a hero by searching endlessly for the "exception" to this rule. If you're willing to bet your business on exceptions you will one day lose it.

4. If other employees have a problem with your investing more of your time and effort on a couple of select people tell them to dry their tears and understand that since your time and energy is limited you're going to distribute it based on "deserve" and not based on "need." You're running a business, not a social service.

5. During employee reviews, don't simply review the numbers someone is producing, but spend more time looking at how they're getting them. Reinforce the good and redirect the wrong behaviors to keep the person on the right track.

6. Get off your throne often enough to become an effective student of your organization's culture, behaviors, and disciplines. In this way, you'll never have to guess

where the numbers are headed and can preempt performance shortfalls.

7. Keep the numbers in their proper perspective but always remember that they are lagging indicators. Don't relegate yourself from leader to analyst by becoming seduced by numbers-crunching when instead you should be obsessed with your people's behaviors.

8. If you have employees who generate the numbers but compromise your values the blind eye you turn will become a black eye when they—and you—are caught compromising the game for the scoreboard. It's okay to be a bit skeptical, a bit paranoid, and a bit more curious about how your people are performing their job. Failing to do so is not only negligent—it's naïve.

9. I hope you realize that the profiling techniques I've given you in this chapter are pure gold. They're worth far more than the price of this book, so if you're feeling that you've taken advantage of me and want to make things right I recommend you send a check for any amount you deem appropriate to:

The Dave Anderson Corporation
P.O. Box 2338
Agoura Hills, CA 91376

Make the check out to EQUIP, which is my favorite ministry that you'll read more about in Chapter 10. We'll both feel better as a result and the folks at EQUIP will put it to good use training Christian leaders around the world.

CHAPTER

4

Sometimes You Have to Tick People Off!

Peering into the PC Cesspool

In her book, *The Language Police* (Knopf, 2003), Diane Ravitch documents an extensive list of words, usages, stereotypes, and topics banned by major publishers of educational materials and by state agencies. In case you're still not convinced the world has overdosed on PC palaver, here's more proof.

Abnormal: Banned as demeaning to persons with disabilities. *Sorry, but anyone with two noses or three eyes is abnormal.*

Adam and Eve: Replace with Eve and Adam, to demonstrate that males do not take priority over females. *I'm certain God is grateful the Language Police have corrected His mistake.*

Crazy, crazy person: Banned as offensive; replace with "person with an emotional disability or mental impairment." *Sorry, but when you listen to Ozzy Osbourne speak, it's easier to say he just sounds crazy.*

Fairy: Banned because it suggests homosexuality; replace with "elf." *This could sure get confusing. If one were not paying close attention he might come to believe that there is a movement to constitutionally ban the marriage of Santa's helpers.*

Freshman: Banned as sexist. Replace with "first-year student." *If you're banning "freshman" go ahead and ban "senior," too, because I'm sure someone, somewhere won't like the fact that it refers to someone in their final year.*

Inspirational: Banned as patronizing when referring to a person with disabilities. *Fine, then give me a better word to describe the late Christopher Reeve.*

Snowman: Banned; replace with "snowperson." *Now they've really gone too far. Emasculating Frosty crosses the line.*

Yacht: Banned as elitist. *So it's okay to teach our kids to work hard and one day reward themselves with a rubber raft, but not a yacht? Yea, that will motivate them.*

Business Lesson: It's time to get back to telling it like it is. If someone is fired because they didn't live your values, say so. This will make your values real to everyone else in the organization. If someone is failing, tell them. Don't let them live in a gray area, assuming all is well. If someone is outstanding, tell them that, too, without regard to hurting the feelings of those who didn't earn the compliment. When you sugarcoat the truth, with "he left to explore other opportunities" rather than the honest answer: "He was terminated for nonperformance" you weaken your culture and excuse slothfulness. If I had my way, severance pay would be eliminated for anyone terminated for nonperformance. Business leaders give it out of guilt because they have to fire a sluggard when, if the world was truly just, we'd be handing the loser an invoice for the cost of his or her poor production on the way out the door.

The Art of Honest Feedback

Colin Powell nailed the essence of making waves and politically incorrect leadership when he said: "Being responsible sometimes means pissing people off."[1]

Don't read more into Powell's quote than is there. Politically incorrect leaders don't tick people off through intimidation, other forms of abuse, or by being arrogant jerks; in fact, it's not fair to bring Donald Trump into this. Instead, they tick people off by expecting a lot, giving brutally honest feedback on performance, and holding others accountable for results. And there is no question: The workplace is populated with clods and louts that don't like these traits of politically incorrect leadership! But if you're not ticking people off from time to time by executing these three disciplines then you're not leading effectively. Pathetically, some leadership wimps score a zeppelin-sized zero in these three areas, and breed a pack of worthless workplace wienies that anonymously gimp through their career thinking they're up to par when they're actually a triple bogey.

Giving honest feedback doesn't mean you shout, stomp, or swear. Jesus would enrage the Pharisees and other religious experts of His day by calling them "broods of vipers" and "white-washed tombs." However, the Bible never indicates that He yelled these phrases, nor did He sprinkle His invectives with profanity. He merely spoke from the heart and told it like it was; an art that has gone AWOL in recent years.

In his book, *Coaching for Improved Work Performance* (McGraw-Hill, 2000), Ferdinand Fournies estimates that 50 percent of all performance problems are the result of poor or deficient feedback. During rampant politically correct times, when managers are even more loath to tell it like it is, you can safely say the 50 percent factor soars. Chapter 1 explained how politically incorrect leaders keep people out of

94

a gray area with feedback. It outlined the four keys to feed-back as follows:

1. It happens quickly after performance.
2. It is consistent.
3. It is brutally honest.
4. It is specific.

In this chapter we'll cover five types of feedback: Three are productive and must be leveraged to trigger and support great performances, while the other two are devastating, per-petrated by leadership louses that mistake their leadership title with being a real leader. As you read this chapter be ma-ture enough to recognize where you've screwed up in the past and resolve to cease persisting in such nonsense.

Five Types of Feedback

1. Positive feedback: A form of positive reinforcement that acknowledges good performances. Unfortunately, many managers are stingy with positive feedback and occasionally, while consulting in a business or answer-ing questions at a seminar, I am confronted with one of the dumbest, most devastating phrases a leader can throw up:

   "Why should I tell them they're doing a good job when they're just doing what I'm paying them to do?"
   This drivel reveals a glaring ignorance of human nature

and here's why: Behavioral science teaches that performances that get reinforced, recognized, or rewarded get repeated. Thus, if someone is doing a good job and you want to see more of it, you must reinforce, recognize, or reward it. Simple, right? Then what a travesty that so many leaders adopt the backward, caveman, and prideful posture presented in the aforementioned quote. Why should you reinforce, recognize, or reward productive performances? Because it's the right thing to do—and it works. And quite frankly, that's all you need to know about it.

Some leadership blowhards think that if they give positive reinforcement it will go to people's heads and they'll let up. This is true—for about 5 percent of people! For the other 95 percent, positive reinforcement gives a higher standard to live up to and a fear of letting the person down that bestowed the compliment. It is completely irresponsible—to say nothing of just plain dumb—to debilitate the vast majority of employees because a few loafers might get lazy if you pat them on the back. The answer is to replace the loafers, not to punish the stars. I don't know about you, but when someone compliments me it doesn't cause me to coast. On the contrary, it gives me something to live up to and makes me strive to do even better next time, so I don't disappoint the person whose favor I've gained. I suspect most people feel the same way.

But when someone does a great job and is only told how much better they could have done, apathy and indifference rips out their passion. After all, if nothing is ever going to be good enough, why kill yourself to get results? When an employee starts to expect the worst from his or her boss and is not reinforced, recognized, or rewarded for doing a great job, he or she loses passion, and when passion is lost he or she

96

plateaus. There is nothing wrong with pointing out additional opportunities to employees as long as you've brought closure to the good things they've already achieved. In fact, if you do so, they'll be more open to your input when you do give suggestions. But when they are never acclaimed and only assailed you create a disconnect that drains their drive.

Shamefully, many managers give more positive reinforcement to their pets than to their people. They'll pat their dog on the head but won't pat a human being on the back. Think about how people talk to their pets and compare that to how they interact with most people, and you'll see the problem: "You're such a good boy! I'm so proud of you boy! Daddy loves his big boy!" It's sick! If we'd talk to our people like we talked to our dogs, our people would run through walls for us! (However, I don't suggest those *exact* words are appropriate.)

I also hear the excuse from bosses that all their people talk about and focus on is getting more money, so why bother complimenting a bunch of greedy grunts anyway? But think about this: In the absence of being told you're doing a good job or feeling appreciated or affirmed, money becomes a psychological reparation. It's all someone has to focus on in order to validate why they are staying at their sorry workplace and laboring for such a band of ingrates.

Thus, managers oftentimes unwittingly focus their people on wanting more money—the external rewards—by failing to give these people the more important intrinsic fulfillment they expect from their work. Here's a wake-up call: Most employees are not corporate gigolos and Jezebels that are in it strictly for the money. They want and need the internal satisfaction of doing a great job, and if you're too clueless to give it to them they'll find a leader with a brain and heart that will.

Politically correct patsies are reluctant to single someone out for positive reinforcement because it may seem partial, or to isolate employees not getting the same acclaim. "I wouldn't want to hurt Sorry Suzie's feelings by telling Jane she did a great job or giving her an extra perk." This is politically correct crapola. Give people what they earn and deserve. If they're great tell them so, and if they're failing let them know. This honest and just behavior is the most fair way to deal with your people.

Try as you may, you can't defy human nature. Human beings are wired to perform better when they are reinforced for what they do—period. Understand this or continue to miss the mark of what could be and should be in your organization. In fact, if you continue in an errant leadership style that withholds good while it demands more effort from the abused you will find that more than ever before, your employee will not respond to your style of leadership. Frankly, if there were such a thing as corporate friendly fire, you'd best get some body armor.

Times have changed. Employees have higher expectations, are more educated, and look for more meaning from their work than at any time in history. This is the age of the free agent. People are much more willing to change jobs, and to do so more often. They're much more eager to tell you to "shove it" than in the past. Wake up or you'll become a victim of the war for talent. It's just a matter of time, because there does come a time when enough is enough. If you are a leader who intentionally withholds positive reinforcement I sincerely hope you lose your best people. This will accomplish two objectives: (1) Lose enough great people and eventually you may lose your own job, which would be just desserts. (2) The departed employees will have a chance of finding a real job in a real workplace with a real leader and reach their potential. In other words, you'll both get what you deserve.

Hard-Charging Strategies

1. Positive feedback is the most cost-effective way to improve performance and motivate your people. Yep, the best way to give your people a raise without having to change their pay plan is to make them more productive. And by giving faster, more consistent, and specific feedback to reinforce the things they do well you will lead them to do more of those productive things. As a result of their improved performance and productivity they will give themselves a raise at the same time as they become more valuable to the company.

2. Even if your own boss doesn't give you positive reinforcement you must do better and do what is right. Just because you have a witless simpleton for a boss, don't compound his or her error by duplicating their incompetence in your own leadership style.

3. Neutral feedback: This simple and direct feedback brings a behavior or performance problem to an employee's attention. This is the first step in addressing the wrong behavior and then following up with a performance expectation. Neutral feedback doesn't have to be

more complicated than the following and should be said respectfully, casually, or firmly:

"John, do you realize that when you show up late for a meeting that you create a distraction and disrespect everyone in attendance? *Could you begin coming in on time starting with next Monday's meeting?*"

All you did in this example was to point out a performance problem and follow it with a desired expectation. You don't have to shout, curse, or demean. Use a conversational yet firm tone; this is all it takes to get the attention of most good performers and let them know you mean business. On the other hand, failing to confront the issue, especially with habitual offenders, invites more of the same deficient results, since you failed to confront the behavior with neutral feedback. Other examples of neutral feedback are:

"Frank, do you know that when you criticize others in public, you disrespect them and make yourself look small? *Could you start counseling these folks privately from today forward?*"

"Betty, are you aware that employees are complaining about your profane, sarcastic remarks in public? *Could you eliminate the dirty language and present yourself in a more professional manner?*"

By bringing the issue to one's attention and defining what you expect, in place of the poor behavior, you keep your people out of a gray area and create a benchmark for future accountability. This lets your people know that you care about their performance and that you're also paying attention to it.

Here are a few examples of effective feedback used by some of the politically incorrect leaders featured throughout this book:

Coach Vince Lombardi:
"If I ever hear any man on this squad use the words, "nigger," "dago" or other derogatory racial slurs, you're through with this team. I won't stand for that."[2]

After a bad practice
"If you don't do better tomorrow, then you're not going to get Sunday off. Nothing says you have to have a day off. I give a day off and if you don't perform you don't get a day off."[3]

To LeRoy Caffey:
"Lee Roy, if you cheat on the practice field, you'll cheat in the game. If you cheat in the game, you'll cheat the rest of your life. I'll not have it. . . . Lee Roy, you may think I criticize you too much, a little unduly at times. You have the size, the strength, the speed, the mobility, everything in the world nec-essary to be a great football player, except one thing: you're too lazy!"[4]

Jesus:
"Woe to you scribes and Pharisees, hypocrites! For you cleanse the outside of the cup and dish, but inside they are full of extortion and self-indulgence. Blind Pharisee, first cleanse the inside of the cup and dish, that the outside of them may be clean also."[5]

"When you are invited by anyone to a wedding feast, do not sit down in the best place. . . . But when you are invited, go and sit down in the lowest place. . . . For whoever exalts himself will be humbled and he who humbles himself will be exalted.[6]

"When you give a dinner or a supper, do not ask your friends, your brothers, your relatives nor rich neighbors, lest they also invite you back, and you be repaid. But when you give a feast, invite the poor, the maimed, the lame, the blind. And you will be blessed because they cannot repay you: for you shall be repaid at the resurrection of the just."[7]

3. Constructive feedback: points out deficiencies in performance and provides solutions on how to improve. Too many managers are hooked on should-bes. "You should be setting more appointments," "You should be closing more sales," "You should be able to run those reports," "You should be getting more referrals," and the preaching goes on ad nauseam. The fact is that it doesn't take a whole lot of brains or leadership to sit on your haunches and should-be all over yourself. And chances are that your people know what they should be doing but haven't had adequate training or feedback on how to do it well. Stop preaching and start teaching. Constructive feedback ditches the hot air and shows people what good performance looks like, because people would rather see a sermon than hear one. Constructive feedback says: "Let's call the customer and I'll show you how to set the appointment," "Come out with me and I'll show you how to close the sale," "Sit right here and take

notes while I show you how to run the reports," and "Bring me to the customer that you just sold and I'll show you how to ask for the referral." Frankly, many managers spew should-bes because it's been so long since they actually did anything they can't credibly walk their talk.

Following is my favorite example of constructive feedback courtesy of General George S. Patton, facing a group of physical fitness-reluctant senior officers. He breaks a couple of rules in the process . . . but there was a war on!

We are in a long war against a tough enemy. We must train millions of men to be soldiers! We must make them tough in mind and body, and they must be trained to kill. As officers we will give leadership in becoming tough physically and mentally. Every man in this command will be able to run a mile in fifteen minutes with a full military pack including a rifle! We will start running from this point in exactly thirty minutes!

One of the overweight senior officers then chuckled.

Damn it! Patton shouted, *I mean every man of this command. Every officer and enlisted man—staff and command; every man will run a mile! We will start running from this point in exactly thirty minutes! I will lead!*

The equivalent would be a general sales manager saying:

We are in a competitive war. We've got to train our team to make more sales. We need to make them disciplined and persistent. As their leaders, we'll set the tone by performing the skills we demand of them with perfection. Every manager on this team will be able to recite every closing technique we teach these men and women and also fluently recite the features, advantages, and benefits of each product we sell. We will begin getting more personally involved with our sales teams by helping them close their deals, calling back their prospects to confirm appointments, and occasionally waiting on prospects to set the example. We will no longer manager our team. We will lead it, and I will start off tomorrow by waiting on the first customer personally.[8]

Don't think you have to give neutral or constructive feedback every single time an employee displays a behavioral or performance short-circuit. Ask yourself, "Is it worth my time?" In other words, if the model employee who is never late to work comes in late one day, you may do more damage to your relationship than good by confronting him or her with his or her tardiness. Or if your most accurate clerk turns in a report with one more mistake than normal you must consider whether it is worth your time to show her how to do it the right way. In other words, don't turn from leader to a nit-picky pest.

Use common sense and your leadership intuition to know when and how often to correct and confront. Otherwise you'll become a major distraction and nuisance while you diminish relationships with your best people and waste both your time. I see too many managers engage in this type of micromanagement of their best people, and it makes me wonder why there aren't more reports of bosses getting their butts kicked by worn-out and frustrated employees.

4. Empty feedback: when good or poor performance takes place and no feedback at all is given. Leaders who engage in empty feedback are more than just negligent. They're lazy. They're clueless bordering on worthless. Needless to say, you must avoid this leadership fault at all costs, because it will asphyxiate your culture.

In the case of empty feedback, good performances are extinguished, since you fail to reinforce them, and poor performances are tacitly reinforced, since you fail to confront them. Thus it is a primary demotivator for solid performers, since they are never acknowledged, while at the same time they see the lollers getting by with impotent and often corrupt efforts. Empty feedback is often the work of isolated, out-of-touch leaders. These lumps spend more time in their office with paperwork than out in the trenches engaged in people work. Thus, they're not around to pat the backs when things go well or to kick the butts when things get off-track. As a result, their culture slumbers, behavior diminishes, and productivity disappears. To call these people leaders is a lie, because at this stage they no longer lead anyone nor add value to anything; they merely preside. They are ceremonial leaders at best and should be expeditiously removed from their positions.

5. Negative feedback. Negative feedback comments are normally put-downs or name-calling rather than useful exchanges of information. Many managers engage in the corporate version of this nonsense simply because they can: In other words, they abuse their au-

thority by intimidating underlings who can do little to fight back.

Needless to say, negative feedback cheapens and diminishes the person spewing the bile more than the intended target. At the same time, it humiliates and demeans the subject, oftentimes creating such a distraction they can no longer concentrate on their work and are preoccupied with thoughts of revenge. To good-naturedly joke with a confidant in private is one matter, but to emote negative feedback in anger, to belittle, to demean or to say in public is a serious leadership sin.

To be involved in public confrontations in any capacity is destructive to your leadership. Lesson: Don't argue with a fool, because spectators can't tell the difference. If this sort of interaction with your people is part of your nature you had best work hard to change it. It is not funny and it is not productive. And some day you might just find out the hard way by bullying the wrong person at the wrong time. If so, you'd best hope your benefit package includes generous disability provisions.

Hard-Charging Strategies

1. Neutral, positive, and constructive feedback are coaching tools you must employ consistently, honestly, specifically, and soon after performance. You should also do so professionally, conversationally, and respectfully.

2. Empty feedback is an indictment of poor leadership and labels you a management imposter, whereas negative feedback establishes you as a monster. They both cause the diminishment of people and the debilitation of culture. Avoid them or you become a willing participant in the demise of your team and your own self-destruction as a leader.

3. Negative feedback is the realm of the lowest-level form of leader. If you don't have skills, morals, or talent as a leader it will become your tool of choice. You cannot lead effectively if you are a wise-cracking, abusive, negative leader. If you don't surrender this habit from your leadership arsenal, you're through as a leader. It's just a matter of time.

5

Learn to Read between the Lies!

Peering into the PC Cesspool

Some holidays have been celebrated for centuries: Easter, Christmas, Hanukah, and Kwanzaa. Well, not quite. The politically correct multiculturists in academia, fueled by leftist media hype, have created a universal acceptance for Kwanzaa. In fact, you'd think that Kwanzaa was a legitimate celebration passed down through the generations in Africa and just recently making a splash in Western cultures. In fact, people are reluctant to say "Merry Christmas" during December because they might offend those celebrating Hanukah or Kwanzaa, also celebrated in that month. So rather than stand for something specific, multitudes of politically correct cop-outs use holiday salutations like: "Happy Holidays," or "Seasons Greetings."

Today, you can buy Kwanzaa cards and send Kwanzaa e-greetings; kids are taught about Kwanzaa in their classrooms to promote the beauty of diversity, and in an example of either extreme ignorance or political correctness gone berserk, the Bush White House issued a proclamation celebrating Kwanzaa in 2002 and 2003. So what's the problem in honoring and rejoicing in this long-steeped African tradition of merriment? It's a sham. Kwanzaa was invented in 1966 by an American Marxist, Ron Karenga, while head of the United Slaves Organization, a black power rival of the Black Panthers.[1] Karenga was later sentenced and served 4 years in prison for the assault and torture of two women followers, and was diagnosed as paranoid and schizophrenic while behind bars.[2] Karenga retired in 2002 as chair of the black studies department at Cal State Long Beach where he served and poisoned students' minds for 13 years with his anti-American, racist doctrine.[3] When once asked why he designed Kwanzaa to take place around Christmas, Karenga said, "People think it's African but it's not. I came up with Kwanzaa because Black people wouldn't celebrate it if they knew it was American. Also, I put it around Christmas because I knew that's when a lot of Bloods would be partying."[4]

This phony went on to explain that his creation of Kwanzaa was partly motivated by his hatred of Christianity and Judaism. Thus, when you wish someone a "Happy Kwanzaa," or acknowledge it or celebrate it in any way, not only are you displaying a classic case of moral ignorance; you are legitimizing a hoax designed to fuel hatred and division between the races.

Business Lesson: Don't be a sheep! Learn to read between the lines—the lies—of conventional wisdom and accepted practices: the "Kwanzaas" found throughout society as well as your industry. When dogmas and untruths are espoused often enough, well-intentioned but unthinking people become desensitized to facts, fall prey to groupthink, and begin to embrace the myths en masse. It's time to peer beneath the surface of accepted stereotypes and best practices in both society and business to ensure you are thinking independently and not following the PC herd of sheep off the cliff of significance and into a pit of irrelevance.

Following are three parallels relating to reading between the lies in society and business to help you create the level of independent thought necessary to lead intelligently and make good decisions in the midst of today's PC mire.

Debunking Common Myths and Reading between the Lies

Just as Chapter 3 taught to not look at just the *what* but to become more inquisitive, dig deeper, and examine the *how*, these examples will show how a combination of old-world thinking and politically correct propaganda hides the truth, and teach the importance of being more cynical of conventional wisdom as well as the media—the best business practices and of most of the people you will ever meet on earth. For instance, here are three quick examples of the necessity for making some waves and reading between the lies in both society and business:

Three widely accepted examples of conventional wisdom in society:

1. Widely Accepted Example #1: General George Armstrong Custer was an overrated glory hog.

   Everything I learned about General George Armstrong Custer in school was negative. And Hollywood has done little to dispel those myths. He is portrayed as arrogant, overly ambitious, reckless, and, most offensive to the politically correct crowd, he fought those peaceful Native Americans known as the Sioux. We've all heard of Custer's Last Stand: how this glory-hog of a commander led all 211 of his men to death by taking on the impossible odds of an enemy that numbered in the thousands at the Little Big Horn.

Without a doubt, Custer made miscalculations at Little Big Horn, but what is never mentioned is that the disproportionate number of casualties he and his men inflicted on the Indians prevented them from ever launching another major offensive against western settlers.

What is also conveniently overlooked in history books and movies such as *Gettysburg* is that Custer saved the Union with his heroics on the third day of the Battle of Gettysburg. In fact, I would bet most readers aren't aware that Custer fought at Gettysburg, much less was one of its biggest heroes. After all, contemporary educators and filmmakers wouldn't want to give approbation to someone who did something as reprehensible as fight and kill Indians.

If you're familiar with the battle of Gettysburg you know that on the third and final day of battle the Confederates made a bold and gutsy march up Cemetery Hill to attack Union positions. If the Rebels had broken through the lines they'd have won the battle and would have had a clear path to march south and capture and occupy Washington. What movies like *Gettysburg* and most historical texts fail to mention—and which is why you must learn to read between the lies—is that at the same time General Pickett led his charge up Cemetery Hill to attack the Yankees, Confederate General Robert E. Lee had ordered General J. E. B. Stuart and his cavalry, known as the "Invincibles," to simultaneously strike behind enemy lines and create a pincer movement that would break in half the Union position. Stuart's cavalry earned their nickname "Invincibles" for good reason: They had never lost a battle. The only problem for Stuart and

113

his perfect record that day was a 23-year-old general by the name of Custer, who personally led the outnumbered Union cavalry, known as the Wolverines, in a head-on collision with the Invicibles before they could reach the Union rear. After Custer's horse was shot from underneath him and post taking a bullet, this "overrated glory-hog" mounted another horse and entered the fray. Custer personally felled the Confederate standard-bearer, the Union captured the enemy's flag, and handed Stuart and his no-longer-"Invincibles" a defeat. In his book, *Custer—Favor the Bold* (BBS Publishing, 1994) D. A. Kinsley wrote, "Custer succeeded in turning the tide at Gettysburg by saving Meade from a disastrous rear attack by Stuart."[5]

Custer's heroics in the Civil War didn't begin or end at Gettysburg. He personally led 21 cavalry charges in the Civil War and had 11 horses shot out from under him[6] (which would make him the subject of PETA protests today). If you visit Gettysburg, you can read these words on the field where he saved the day, the battle and, arguably, the country: "This monument marks the field where the Michigan Cavalry Brigade, under its gallant leader, General George Custer, rendered signal and distinguished service in assisting to defeat the further advance of a numerically superior force under Confederate General J. E. B. Stuart who, in conjunction with Pickett's Charge upon the center, attempted to turn the right flank of the Union Army at the critical hour of the conflict on the afternoon of July 3, 1863."

As Paul Harvey says, "now you know the rest of the story" behind a man left out of documentaries, movies, and textbooks because later in his career he killed Indians: An unforgivable and very politically incorrect act in this CNN age of "blame America first and everything American while you're at it."

2. Widely Accepted Example #2: George W. Bush is stupid.

During the 2000 presidential race, candidate Al Gore was deemed so smart as to be out of touch with average Americans. At least his superior intellect was blamed for his failure to connect with many Americans. (Gee, and I thought it was his whiney, boring speeches.) Gore was said to grow impatient while conversing with those of lower IQ, and was presented as a scholarly and diligent student. His opponent, Texas governor George W. Bush, was accused of having sailed through school on his father's name, even though at the time Bush senior was a little-known Congressman from Texas on the verge of losing his first Senate race.

Bush, lacking in linguistic prowess, was often parodied as the bumbling bumpkin, too dumb to be president—while the biased media presented Gore as the "smartest kid in his class" in dozens of articles and stories. The only problem was that it wasn't true. In fact, Gore was about as far from the "smartest kid in the class" as he was from being an interesting human being. Vice President Al Gore, both the self-proclaimed inventor of the Internet and the inspiration behind the movie *Love Story*, had school records that were atrocious. In high school he received mostly Cs and Bs in English and history; Cs in French, and the only As he received were in art class. Gore, gaining entrance into Harvard in spite of his grades and with thanks to his prominent senator father, made a splash his sophomore year with one D, two Cs, two C-pluses, and one B.[7]

The *Washington Post* reported that this put him in the bottom fifth of his class for the second year in a row.[8] It also mentioned that Gore's grades that year were lower than any semester recorded on Bush's transcript from Yale.[9]

After Yale, Bush earned an MBA from Harvard (the only president with an MBA); Gore flunked out of divinity school—failing five out of eight classes—and dropped out of law school at Vanderbilt University.[10]

More recently, in the 2004 election, the media once again tried to convince the world that Bush was still stupid and his opponent, Senator John Kerry, was the "smart one." Wrong again. Months after the election, when former candidate Kerry finally agreed to release his Navy records, they showed that during Kerry's four years at Yale his grade point average was worse than Bush's, and included a less-than-illustrious four Ds his freshman year.

Even though he does and says things from time to time that make my jaw drop, I like George W. Bush. But much of the world detests him because he's politically incorrect. He says what's on his mind and he doesn't say it with proper enunciation. He has the audacity to inflict consequences on the cutthroats who attack the country he's been hired to defend. He doesn't kiss the keister of the United Nations or the world's biggest has-been: France. And this ticks people off. Bush is offensive. He is abrupt. He makes unpopular decisions. He isn't polished. He isn't articulate. He's too direct. He's too religious. He unapologetically puts his own country's welfare first, and the rest of the world—and many brainwashed Americans included—hate him for it.

Perhaps you swallowed the media's bait and believed the

lie that Gore was a scholar and Bush was a dunce. You're not alone. But you've got to do better. In your personal and business life you must develop the discipline to read between the lies and develop an adequate level of cynicism that will stop you from being duped, seduced, and reduced to just another unthinking follower in a growing cult of American Stepford clones.

3. Widely Accepted Example #3: The mainstream media is fair and balanced.

If the previous example didn't convince you of this lie, perhaps the following will do the trick:

A survey published by the Media Research Center reported that journalists from outside Washington, D.C. enjoyed a pro-Democrat to Republican majority by a margin of three to one while the ratio of pro-Democrat journalists from Washington, D.C. itself rose to a lopsided 12 to 1! Regardless of your political affiliation, this should alarm you, because how can you expect to hear the truth with a bias of this magnitude?

The same report indicates that Americans are catching on: Since 1985, the percentage of Americans who perceive a liberal bias has doubled from 22 percent to 45 percent, nearly half the adult population. A plurality of Democrats now also admit that the press is liberal.

Journalists need to get out more. They need to realize that there's an entirely different country west of Times Square and Washington, D.C., and east of Beverly Hills.

They're so blinded by their dominant environment they've lost their perspective and objectivity. I'm certain that if your brain is mostly intact you have figured this media bias out on your own over the years; I just thought you'd feel better seeing it validated in writing.

These three examples of deception and defective perception evince the need to think for yourself; to read between the lies; to become more cynical of most everyone and everything—especially if it involves revisionist history taught in schools or the mainstream media. Don't be naive. Don't be a boob. Don't be a sheep. The bad guys are counting on it.

Throughout this book, I have shown the correlation between how trends in business follow those in society. And the workplace today certainly proves the premise of needing to read between the lies in business, because industry is overpopulated today with the unthinking. People are so busy, and the pace of business so quick, that they live their lives at work and at home by instinct; making it up as they go along; by seeing a moving line and getting in it. CEOs and frontline managers alike have become addicted to lethal best practices and archaic conventional wisdom. They merrily follow the herd, and consequently step in what it leaves behind. Here are three examples of widely accepted yet deadly business myths you must divorce from your business psyche:

Conventional Wisdom Business Myth #1: The Most Effective CEOs Are Commanding and Charismatic Figures

Lee Iacocca, Chainsaw Al Dunlap, and Donald Trump come to mind when you think of larger-than-life leaders who are super-successful in leading their organizations to new levels. However, according to Jim Collins' masterpiece, *Good to Great*, the leaders of the companies that made the leap from good to great were led by mostly unassuming leaders you've never heard of—and that's the way these leaders liked it. The brash and flashy CEO could often get results and attention for a while, but rarely built the foundation for sustainable success in their enterprise. Excessive pride and the resulting absent humility was often the cause for the Iacocca-type leaders' roller-coaster ride and unsustainable success.

Despite what conventional wisdom and reality television would have you believe, humility is a key trait of the most successful leaders, and if you aspire to leadership greatness in your organization you must make some personal waves by subordinating your own ego to the good of the team. In fact, I believe that failure to do so is the number one cause of management failure. Let me explain:

There are many reasons managers fail. For some, the organization outgrows them. Others don't change with the times. Others still spread themselves too thin, and work long and hard but not smart. Many abandon the priorities and disciplines that once made them great, and never get back to them. A few make poor character choices. They look good for a while but eventually discover they can't get out of their

119

own way. Increasingly more keep the wrong people too long because they don't want to admit they made a mistake or have high employee turnover become a negative reflection on them. Some failures had brilliant track records but started using their success as a license to build a fence around what they had, rather than continue to risk and stretch to build it to even higher levels. But all these causes for management failure have their root in one common cause: pride. In simplest terms, pride is devastating. Having pride in what you do is not the type of pride I'm referring to. I'm indicting the pride that inflates your sense of self-worth and distorts your perspective of reality.

1. Pride will stop you from building a team. Because you depend too much on yourself you won't trust, delegate to, or give additional opportunities to others. Quite frankly, because of your inflated sense of self-worth you won't really see the need for others. Thus, you'll become the one-man show, micromanaging and limiting others in your charge.

2. Pride renders you unteachable. Your pride tells you that you know it all, and thus you don't commit to personal growth. There's always something better to do with your time and money, and since your ego convinces you that you've arrived and have all the answers, who needs business books, consultants, or seminars?

3. Pride closes your mind to feedback. When others offer you advice or direction you let it go in one ear and out the other and do things your way. Because of your

bloated ego you never seek out feedback that would help you grow, as it could be seen as a sign of weakness.

4. Pride causes you to keep the wrong people too long. Many managers keep obvious misfits on their payrolls because to fire them would be a tacit admission that they made a mistake in the first place, or were unable to develop the person to a higher level. Their pride convinces them if they keep working with the miserable that one day they can elevate them up to mediocre.

5. Pride will prevent you from admitting mistakes on one hand while it encourages you to take all the credit on the other. Thus, you will teach others to cover their own behinds by virtue of your own corrupt example, and never build an open, trusting environment. Even worse, you're likely to take out your black belt in blame when things go wrong and point to others in order to take the spotlight off you. At the same time, you'll hog the credit when things go well, and set a selfish standard followers will emulate.

6. Pride will cause you to pledge allegiance to the status quo rather than be open to change, especially if the change alters something you put in place. Since you have more emotional equity in the way things are, you'll justify living with them rather than changing them.

7. Pride encourages poor character choices. Because of arrogance, ignorance, or a little of both, you start taking shortcuts that compromise your values. In your conceit you think you're above the rules or are too smart to get caught.

To further expose the dangers of pride, in my book, *Up Your Business*, I outlined the Six Temptations of Successful Organizations. In condensed form they are:

1. The leaders of successful organizations stop working on themselves.
2. The leaders of successful organizations stop thinking big.
3. The leaders of successful organizations stop leading from the front.
4. The leaders of successful organizations stop developing others.
5. The leaders of successful organizations stop holding others accountable.
6. Everyone in successful organizations abandons the basics.

Pride is at the root of each of these temptations. In the first Temptation, pride makes you unteachable. In the second, it causes you to believe you've arrived. In the third, pride diverts your attention from people work to paperwork, since people are messier and more troublesome to deal with than safe and sterile administration. In the fourth Temptation, pride causes you to become too dependent on yourself, and not to see the need to invest in others. After all, you're there, so who needs others? In the fifth Temptation, you believe that because of your own genius the good times will last forever, and you begin losing the urgency to confront and turn around deficient performances. You somehow believe the havoc poor performers inflict on other companies in the marketplace doesn't apply to you. Thus, like the captain of the *Titanic*, you walk around straightening deck chairs rather than feeling the urgency that would make you change course. And in the sixth Temptation, you think that you've outgrown the daily and weekly disciplines that got you to where you are, and you spend your time looking for faster and fancier strategies. Let's face it—success is an intoxicant, and intoxicated people don't think clearly or face reality very well.

Jim Collins' research went on to show that the leaders of the great companies maintained a strong personal humility balanced with a ferocious ambition for the organization. This is an optimal recipe for great leaders. It's fine to be proud of your business, abilities, and accomplishments. But when pride causes you to fall into any of these traps it won't be long until you're finished as a leader. You don't have to look far to see how pride has wreaked havoc on leaders from all walks; destroying Enron, imprisoning Jim Bakker, deluding Saddam, and tarnishing Iacocca.

Proverbs indicates that pride comes before destruction, and lists pride as the first of seven things God hates. I don't know about you, but that certainly gets my attention. Too many people think that ancient, proven, and universal laws somehow don't apply to them; that they're different or above what the rest of us must pay attention to. They are dead wrong. We all may fall into prideful traps from time to time. It comes with the territory of being a flawed human being. But failing to recognize the error and change your course is what finishes you as a leader, because pride is a character flaw, and leaders that last and leave legacies have their character intact. This prediction of demise is not a guess—it's a guarantee. It's not a matter of if but of when. There are no exceptions.

If pride hinders you it's time to face it and begin to humble yourself before the marketplace does it for you. Humility doesn't mean you think less of yourself; it just means you think of yourself less. If pride is infecting your people don't pretend it isn't happening. Care enough to confront them with it. Letting them live in denial is dangerous, because they will continue to misdiagnose everything wrong with their business and their life. Until they acknowledge how pride holds them back they will never change. If all else fails, remind them or yourself of the brilliant quote by Charles Spurgeon: "Success can go to my head and will unless I remember that it is God who accomplishes the work, that he can continue to do so without my help and that he will be able to make out with other means whenever he wants to cut me out."

Hard-Charging Strategies

1. If you do have strong charismatic qualities realize that they can work against you, because people may be less anxious to challenge you, give you constructive feedback, or tell you what you really need to hear.

2. Never forget that you're not the Center of the Universe. That job is already taken.

3. Realize that the moment you're ready to write it down, produce the manual, and document the formula is the day you put yourself on the endangered species list. Develop the discipline and humility to come to work and prove yourself over again each day.

4. Accept the fact that bragging, show-boating, and arrogance are premier turn-offs to followers. They can also cause you to make a spectacle of yourself, as Donald Trump did when he proclaimed, in an *Esquire* magazine interview titled, "How I'd Run the Country Better" how he'd do a better job running the country than President Bush—just weeks before his casinos officially filed for bankruptcy.

5. You don't need Brioni suits, a Rolex watch, or a Harvard MBA to be a dynamic and effective leader in your organization. In fact, there are plenty of pretenders sporting all three who have led their organizations to ruin. Nor do you need white skin, male gender, a heterosexual orientation, or to attend a Protestant or Catholic church. What you need is character, competence, and consistency. And if you are *the* leader, these are the traits you should be looking for in others. Ditch your stereotyped image of what a "leader" is supposed to look or sound like. Leadership is a personal choice; leadership is influence; leadership is performance, not position. You either get this or you don't, and if you don't, you're hopeless.

Conventional Wisdom Business Myth #2: Bigger Is Better—The Higher Our Revenues the More Successful We've Become

This myth has been perpetuated since the beginning of business time. Everyone wants to expand, to acquire, and to increase sales, because it proves they're growing and successful. What a crock! The major airlines' revenues increased for years, and more major carriers are either in, emerging from, or teetering on the edge of bankruptcy than ever before. Why? Their business model and cost structure stinks! Pursuing revenues is like a drug: It's an ego-driven addiction that creates the mirage of growth. You can double your sales and still go broke if you don't have profits. And oppositely to what some imbeciles in boardrooms seem to think, revenues don't necessarily mean profits. You can have both increased revenues and higher profits, but, contrary to conventional wisdom that says "get bigger at any cost," the profits should be pursued and secured first.

Consider the following:

Many businesses have done an adequate job in recent years of growing their enterprise horizontally, by adding new profit centers to existing points or through buying competitors who inflate their revenue portfolio. As important as horizontal growth through acquisitions can be to your business, it is often a greater indicator of your credit line than your business leadership. A truer test of business acumen is whether you can grow your organization vertically; line-by-line increases in gross dollar sales, unit sales, net profit, and the like. Another question is that if you are growing profits, is it because of real top-line growth or just because you've gotten better at cost cutting? There's no question that it's easier to cut the buck than expand the bang, but to achieve sustainable profits that increase steadily over time you must earn top-line growth—because as important as cost cutting is, it eventually brings a diminished return.

Frankly, it's easier to achieve increased revenues via horizontal growth than it is to grow profits vertically. In fact, it's a quick-fix for the ego: you can exhibit visible signs of growing even though you may have substituted acquisition for execution. Let's face it: hiring extra bodies, adding new departments and buying other businesses—"doing deals"—can be a lot more fun than exercising the daily discipline and accountability required to structure your business for maximum profit, maximize current resources, and grow vertically. The payoff of pursuing profits first is that the structure you create better positions you to chase horizontal revenues and expand your business. Contrary to the seductive appeal and conventional wisdom that says "grow through acquisition," following are four cautions on relying too much on acquisitions and expansion to grow your business.

1. Acquisitions can distract you. They can take your focus away from building your core business and spread you and your resources too thin. Acquisitions are seductive. It's far more exciting to buy something than to dig deep and maximize your current business assets and opportunities.

2. When you rely on acquisitions for growth and spread valuable resources thin without a supporting profit structure, one bad move, two bad months, or paying too much for a new entity makes your entire operation vulnerable, as there is little margin for error before a financial squeeze becomes a hangman's noose.

3. Acquisitions tempt you to chase revenues over profits. The problem is that without being structured for profit in your business, the additional revenues become a mirage, disappearing through the sieve of a foundation built on sand. Again, while you can have both revenues

and profits, focus on pursuing profits first, because until you are structured for profit by virtue of a sensible expense structure, sound systems and controls, and a maximization mindset to execute current opportunities, revenues won't sustain your enterprise. Besides, you shouldn't be interested in having one big sale after another just to exchange four quarters for a dollar.

Profits are the lifeblood of business, and once you have them you can then venture into sensible acquisitions, but a profit structure must come first. The old mantra, "We'll lose money on each unit but make it up on volume" is an excuse for the inability to execute, and a financial death wish without a supporting profit structure.

4. Acquisitions can dilute your talent pool. Unless you have a strong bench of leaders you've developed, acquisitions spread your talent too thin, jeopardizing the "mother cow" that made the acquisition possible in the first place.

Some will argue that cash flow is more immediately important than profits, but without a profit structure, sound accounting practices, turning inventories fast, funding finance contracts quickly, and tightening up receivables, your cash flow quickly disappears.

Frankly, it's time for some leaders to park their egos, stop playing J. R. Ewing, and get back to growing their business vertically, from the inside, before their horizontal empire turns into a quagmire. While buying the next business temporarily takes the pressure off having to maximize your current assets and opportunities, there does come a day of reckoning. This day arrives at the worst possible time, and seems to come out of nowhere, even though it has gradually built up a head of steam over time. Suddenly your failed discipline, loose systems, loss of focus, depletion of resources, absent accountability, and inability to grow others begins to manifest itself in the form of a plateau, gradual decline, or outright plummet.

Hard-Charging Strategies

Here are four tips to strengthen your own profit structure, positioning you for maximum returns. Once this structure is in place, you'll have the financial fuel to chase revenues through acquisition and expand horizontally, creating sustainable growth and long-term financial vitality for your businesses.

1. *Instill financial discipline and tighten cash flow procedures, since it's not what you make—it's what you keep—that counts.* If there is one area in your business where it's appropriate to micromanage, it is your financial systems and controls; maintaining sensible inventories and turning them quickly, collecting receivables, getting contracts funded, controlling expenses, remaining right-sized, and the like. Set clear expectations for results in each of these areas and meticulously manage the details necessary to optimize them.

2. *Create systems and mindsets that maximize current opportunities and assets.* Most businesses don't need additional opportunities. They need only to maximize those they

waste each day in order to send results soaring. Spending more and more on advertising is like a shot of morphine that temporarily deadens your pain and hides the fact that your managers are doing a lousy job of managing current opportunities; thus they look to you to buy them more. Morphine is addictive, and too much of it can kill you. Eventually you need to stop deadening the pain and have surgery, and the same goes for your business. Other assets that you must maximize are your incoming phone calls and your customer base. In most businesses the management of both these sectors is beyond sloppy; it's atrocious.

3. *Focus managers on growing their teams vertically first, then horizontally.* The truest measure of a manager is whether they can improve and develop their people. When most managers want to increase sales they hire more people rather than develop the ones they have. This "hire three more guys" mentality presupposes your current employees are maxed out. Hiring more people rather than making current employees better is not effective leadership; it's surrender. The trench warfare mentality—throw bodies at the problem and maybe we'll get results—should be an indictable offense. Hold your managers more personally responsible for the individual improvement of each person on their team. If they can't get people consistently and measurably better, either train your managers, demote them, or fire them and get some real help.

4. *Begin an acceleration pool—an inner circle—of upcoming talent.* You'll never have the depth to pursue vertical

growth or sustain horizontal growth, or staff new profit centers or new businesses, until you start building a bench—an acceleration pool of talent—before the need arises. Every growing organization needs a mentoring program that identifies upcoming talent and systematically and deliberately builds their knowledge and skill capacity. Until you begin to develop leaders at all levels in your organization you are essentially immobilized, and cannot consistently grow vertically, much less even think about acquisitions. The profiling techniques presented in Chapter 3 will address this need.

Take a second look at your growth strategy and determine if you've been seduced by acquisition and expansion. Maybe it's time to get back to the basics of sound business. Are you structured for maximum profit? Are you building a bench? And if not, what are you waiting for?

Conventional Wisdom Business Myth #3: Everyone on the Team Is Mostly Unselfish and Wants What's Best for the Team

If you believe this conventional wisdom someone should make you submit to a drug test. Regardless of your champagne wishes and caviar dreams, most teams are still populated by imperfect, selfish, insecure, and oftentimes spiteful human beings who spend more time stabbing than patting one another's backs. Just because the back-stabbing and jockeying for position isn't blatant doesn't mean it's not happening: Read between the lines and the lies to reveal what's really taking place in your organization. When one of your "one for all and all for one" team members approaches you with an idea, suggestion, or strategy, remove your cataracts and determine the following.

Hard-Charging Strategies

1. Consider the source. What personal gain does the person promoting the idea have at stake? The "motives test" reveals more frauds than anything else. Since past performance is the best predictor of future performance you should also recall if the issues raised by this person in the past have been for the betterment of the team or for him- or herself.

2. Beware of general statements like: "It's a well-known fact that . . ." or "Numerous studies show that . . ." or "The general consensus is that . . ." Don't accept general fluff espoused by blowhards too lazy to do their homework, and who take you for a fool who will accept their shoot-from-the-hip style without a deeper investigation and pointed questions, like "On what basis do you regard what you're telling me is a well-known fact," or "Please name or provide for me the studies which you cite," or "Specifically, to which studies do you refer?" By slowing down a hyped-up onslaught of pomposity you will likely uncover an argument built on the sands of emotion and self-interest and without factual basis, and you will teach people to get their facts straight before they try and give you another enema of their biased blather.

132

3. Don't make an immediate decision or commitment on what is obviously an emotional argument presented by an employee. Slow down the momentum of passion brought on by hysterical charges and claims by asking questions as suggested in Point 2, and taking the time to do your own investigating before rendering an opinion or decision. Too many leaders let others work them up into such a frenzy with outrageous claims and charges that they make stupid and reckless statements or commitments, and come to regret them immediately thereafter.

4. If you suspect someone's comments are a subtle attempt to bury a hatchet in another employee's torso, shift the focus of the conversation by suggesting: "Rather than talk *about* this person, what do you say we both go and talk *to* this person to get matters resolved?" You'll quickly learn the true motives of Mr. or Mrs. Helper.

5. Don't despise those with whom you disagree. When I was younger I didn't get this. I resented, looked down upon, and many times despised those who had the audacity to disagree with me. But one day I wised up and realized: If someone has legitimately thought out his or her opinion, done the homework, and can make a compelling argument for his or her point of view, it is worth my time to listen and learn—even if I don't agree. The people I now have no tolerance for are those who don't have an opinion; the unthinking souls who bumble through life reacting and improvising while others think for them; the timid little gnats that can't or won't take a stand because they are uninformed or just so plain stupid they can't outwit a lab rat.

We must not be in Kansas anymore, Toto. After all, if you can't trust conventional wisdom and best practices, then what or whom can you trust? I mean, if the best leaders don't really look like Dapper Dan and swagger through the corridors with minions swooning over their charisma; and if getting bigger isn't necessarily better; and if not everyone on the team really cares about putting the team first, where should our cynicism end? It shouldn't. In fact, the moment you lose your curiosity and cease asking questions and digging deeper, stop doing your homework and thinking independently about society and business issues, you're little better than barnyard critters and wild beasts, whose high points in life are to sleep and eat while they survive on instinct rather than intellect.

CHAPTER 6

Ditch Diversity and Go for Results!

Peering into the PC Cesspool

In 2003, the Supreme Court issued two rulings concerning the University of Michigan's affirmative action admission programs. The freedom to violate the Constitution and continue discriminating against whites, Arab-Americans, and Asian-Americans, among others, was upheld overall, but the court did strike down the school's corrupt practice of awarding twenty points toward admission (out of 150 total needed) to African American, Hispanic, and Native American applicants. To put this practice in perspective it's important to know that the same admission system that gave away 20 points for genetics awarded only 12 points for a perfect SAT score!

According to proponents, the goal of this discrimination is a more diverse classroom, which they claim results in a better education. This is a classic liberal lie. No study exists that proves the student in a more diverse classroom gets a better education than the kid in a less diverse setting. Point-systems like the one outlawed are blatant examples of giving someone something because of who he or she is rather than for what he or she's done. And in layman's terms, that is exactly what affirmative action does. This practice also demeans the recipient, because it says, in effect, "You're inferior. You can't make it on your own."

How does this affect your business? Without conscious intent, countless corporate leaders have found ways to institute versions of affirmative action in their businesses, where people are rewarded, recognized, and promoted based on who they are rather than on past accomplishments. As a leader, it's vital that you evaluate your own practices in this regard. You may not have considered the following examples as versions of corporate affirmative action, but they are and must be addressed and corrected to build a vibrant business culture.

Versions of Corporate Affirmative Action and How to Overcome Them

1. The most obvious example of corporate affirmative action is where racial preferences and quota mentalities prevail and pressure leaders to rationalize the hiring or promotion of substandard job candidates to create a more diverse workforce. Question: what good does it do you to have a workforce whose ethnicity mimics the United Nations if people aren't competent and can't get the job done? Without a doubt, diversity without competence is worthless. If the best person for the job is a Protestant male whiter than Casper the Friendly Ghost, he should get the job.

If, on the other hand, the most qualified candidate is named Patel, Nguyen, Wong, Mohammed, or Jose, is Jewish, is a lesbian, in a wheelchair, hails from the Congo, or possesses any other trait that would rile Archie Bunker, he or she should get the job. If these merit-based assessments offend you, you're a racist, bigot, or worse. I'm not being judgmental, simply discerning.

2. Bearing in mind that the essence of affirmative action is to reward people based on who they are rather than based on the quality of their results, consider how many business leaders execute an affirmative action mentality as pertains to their long-term, "loyal" employees who have retired on the job and have become entitled squatters just marking time and cashing royalty checks from what they did once upon a time. Leaders serious about making waves and creating a meritocracy must challenge their own definition of loyalty.

Too often, loyalty is defined as "an employee who has been with us a long time." Wouldn't this be better defined as tenure or longevity? It certainly doesn't prove loyalty. Have you looked up the word "loyalty" in the dictionary, as I recommended earlier in this book? If so, you found nothing that mentions a length of time that someone has been in your organization. Thus, if your primary definition of loyalty is that someone has shown up at the same place and at the same time for a certain number of years, your definition is misguided. These factors may constitute good attendance, but not necessarily loyalty.

In fact, designating someone as loyal based on this criteria creates a sense of entitlement in long-term employees. Correct me if I'm wrong, but you didn't stop by their house each morning and kidnap and press these tenured employees into service for all those years. And while they were on the job they were paid well, provided benefits, and afforded opportunities to grow and advance. They weren't volunteers.

I mentioned earlier that in a meritocracy, loyalty should be defined as performance; it's about getting results. Loyalty is putting the organization before one's own needs. It's giving more than you take and doing more than expected. Oppositely, one of the greatest disloyalties someone can inflict on their employer is to stop getting results. If you're lucky enough to have an employee that is both tenured and productive, you've got the ultimate employee. But if years in the workplace are your primary criteria for defining a loyal employee, then the one-year employee that happens to be your best performer would not qualify as a loyal worker, based on your definition, simply because he or she hasn't worked for you long enough. This assertion would be ridiculous, as is the practice of classifying someone as loyal based on how many years he or she has cashed your paychecks.

A third example of someone getting something based on who they are rather than based on what they've accomplished—an affirmative action mindset in industry—is abusive nepotism. Nepotism is common in business simply because there are so many family-owned businesses. There is nothing wrong with having family members working within a business. In fact, under the right conditions, benefits outweigh detriments. Where nepotism takes on the cloak of affirmative action is when a family member isn't held to the same high standard of performance, work ethic, and values as other employees; when they benefit precisely because of who they are rather than what they accomplish.

I have met the offspring of entrepreneurs who have taken their parent's business and transformed it to new levels. On the other hand, there are far too many arrogant, spoiled brats in similar positions who are never held accountable, do not lead by example, add value to nothing, and are just plain lazy. If they were not connected to the family they'd have been fired long ago. A productive conversation a senior family member should have with kin coming into the business would sound something like this:

Your title, money, inheritance, or genes do not make you a leader. Leadership is influence and performance. It is earned, not assumed. You earn it when people buy into your character, competence, and consistency. All your name and title does is buy you time: Time to earn followers or to lose them; to get the job done or to blow it. And be clear on this issue: You don't automatically have followers. You have subordinates. How you act as a leader determines whether your subordinates ever turn into followers.

If you lead by personal convenience rather than personal example, people will comply but never commit. If you commit the cause to yourself rather than committing yourself to a cause, you will fail as a leader. To whom much is given, much is required. Thus, you will be held to a higher standard, scrutinized and judged more harshly than anyone else in the company. This comes with the territory. If it sounds unfair or is asking too much, then stay out of my company.

Affirmative Action Doesn't Ensure Fairness: It Destroys It!

As I asserted in the opening pages of the preface, trends in business always follow trends in society. Thus, as affirmative action mindsets and values become more prominent in society they gain validation and credibility in business. And as a result, they destroy the performance-based psyche required to build and sustain great enterprises.

Affirmative action has ill-served its intended benefactors. In fact, it has made them more dependent on outside help and less responsible for their own actions. It has also created a swell of resentment from those not qualifying for the "extra points" that further isolates its intended beneficiaries. In short, affirmative action and like programs are destroying the people they purport to help.

From Bad to Worse

Society's infatuation with weakening the majority to strengthen the underdog doesn't stop with 20-point plus factors and the self-serving antics of shakedown artists. The same mentality has carried over into aspects of everyday life with increasing frequency. Following are just two of the more outrageous examples:

Scenario One: Liberal Society's View of Fairness: In the wake of the World Trade Center massacre, New York City officials wanted to memorialize the now-famous photograph of three firefighters raising an American flag over the rubble and ashes of Ground Zero. Just one problem: All three firefighters were the same race. In order to be "fair," a committee decided to forgo truth for "equality" and erect a 19-foot, $180,000 statue with a more diverse ethnic representation. Kevin James, a spokesman for a minority firefighters' group defending the racially diverse statue declared, "I think the artistic expression of diversity would supercede any concern over factual correctness."[1]

Scenario One: Business Interpretation of Fairness: This example of appeasing racial bean counting is the epitome of political correctness gone nuts. Out-of-the-mainstream society may promote this definition of fairness, but as a business leader you must create another. In case you missed this earlier in the book, in business, treating people fairly doesn't mean you treat them all alike. It means you treat them in a manner they earn and deserve—regardless of race, gender, or creed—and they haven't all earned, nor do they deserve, the same schedule, pay plan, incentives, opportunities, or amount of your time and discretion. Obviously, everyone is held to the same high standard of work ethic, customer care, and integrity. But beyond that, the best businesses distribute resources based on "deserve," not based on "need." While we are all created equally, we don't all create equal value at work. Until leaders get this, and stop trying to make everyone happy in the name of "justice for all," they send the wrong message about expectations, performance, and excellence.

Scenario Two: Liberal Society's View of Fairness: In the wake of the September 11th attacks, undergraduates at Marquette University were blocked from holding a moment of silence around the American flag because of worries it might alienate foreign students; overseers of a cafeteria at Arizona State University had an American flag removed because they feared it might insult foreign students, and officials at the Boulder Public Library refused to hang a 10-foot long

American flag in its lobby, claiming its immigrant patrons might be taken aback.[2] According to the *Denver Post*, while the American flag was deemed too controversial, the library had no problem prominently exhibiting a display of ceramic penises, literally giving our American heritage the shaft.

Scenario Two: Business Interpretation of Fairness: In these incredible examples of pantywaist protocol, common sense would dictate that it is the foreigner's obligation to adjust to our country and culture, not our duty to change for them. Most Americans are proud of their flag, their religious roots, and their capitalistic appetite. Anyone having a problem with these issues is not obligated to remain in the United States. And the same goes for the people in your workplace. As a leader, it's your privilege to set expectations, establish core values, and hold people accountable for making the grade.

Should you listen to others' input and views on these matters? Of course. Effective leaders encourage different points of view and productive dissent. After all, if everyone is thinking alike then someone isn't thinking. But in business, people shouldn't mistake the fact that you give them a voice as the equivalent of your giving them a vote. To run a performance-based enterprise, your concern is not to make people feel safe and secure with a comfortable set of expectations. Your job is to stretch people to your standards, not to lower your standards to accommodate employees. In fact, if your people aren't uncomfortable from time to time they're not growing. You can't grow when you're comfortable. You can only maintain or regress.

A Growing Conga Line of Losers

The problem with society's version of fairness and its devotion to political correctness is that when it carries over into your business you won't face the tough issues. You'll let people live in a gray area. You'll trivialize, rationalize, and marginalize deficient performances for the sake of harmony. You'll become the sultan of sugarcoat and begin hiring, rewarding, and promoting people based on quotas rather than performance. You'll unwittingly encourage people to become victims. This "it's not my fault" mantra has become a national obsession.

Witness the conga line of losers marching into courtrooms to cry victim and sue companies like McDonalds for making them fat. I suppose we're to believe that Ronald McDonald pinned little Waldo to the ground and pummeled him with double cheeseburgers while plunging a vanilla-shake I.V. into his bloated arm.

Are we expected to feel sorry for the countless "I didn't know inhaling tar into my lungs was bad for me" derelicts that have sued tobacco companies for making them sick, and who perpetuate an "It's not my fault" mentality that drifts over and pollutes the workplace? If you don't draw the line, weed out handouts, k.o. the bozos, and edify the eagles in your business, you become a collaborator with the "don't blame me" gaggle of goofballs dedicated to shanghaiing your high-performance business culture.

To reinforce the proper definition of fairness and focus on results over diversity, as highlighted in this chapter, I think it appropriate to include my favorite Vince Lombardi quote: "It is increasingly difficult to be tolerant of a society

144

which seems to have sympathy only for the misfits, only for the maladjusted, only for the criminal, only for the loser. Have sympathy for them, yes; help them, yes; but I think it is also time for us to cheer for, to stand up for, to stand behind the doer; the achiever, the one who recognizes a problem and does something about it, the one who looks for something to do for his country; the winner, the leader."

Can you just imagine the "progressive" version of this, appearing in the op-ed section of the *New York Times* or being hysterically yelled out on a college campus by some wacko professor with a "get the man off our back" tattoo: "The rich and productive citizens of America have betrayed this country! They have too much and we must make it right. We will love the losers, coddle the criminals, and lift up the lazy. We will mend the moochers, defend the derelict, and delight in the depressed. We'll weaken the strong to strengthen the weak, and lower the bar so you get what you need instead of having to settle for what you deserve."

Let's Hear It for Dr. King!

One of history's best spokesmen for merit-based justice was Dr. Martin Luther King, Jr. In his "I Have a Dream" speech he declared, "I have a dream that my four children will one day live in a nation where they will not be judged by the color of their skin but by the content of their character." He did not say, "I have a dream that my four children will one day live in a nation where they will be entitled to a 20-point plus factor based on the color of their skin." When speaking on behalf of African Americans in 1865, the great abolitionist and former slave

Frederick Douglass said, "What I ask for my people is not benevolence, not pity, not sympathy but simply justice. . . . All I ask is to give him a chance to stand on his own legs! Let him alone . . . your interference is doing him positive injury." The same can be said for the "loyal," the blood-related, and the "special case" employees in your business that are not held accountable, not required to perform, and who get away with failing to hit your standards—solely because of who they are. This affirmative action mindset weakens your culture, creates resentment and distractions, and derails your potential.

Abolish your welfare state and establish a meritocracy. You're running a business, not the Good Ship Lollipop. Just because some of today's leaders have hijacked Dr. King's dream and turned it into a nightmare doesn't mean you have to let the same perverse values and standards created by an affirmative action mindset destroy your merit-based mindset or your high performance culture. Black or white, brown or yellow, you can and must do better.

What's Your Excuse, White Boy?

In Jerry Springer circles, the following will go over like a soul food buffet at a Klan reunion, but I've got to get it off my chest. Of all the underachieving losers in the world today I can't think of a bigger clunker in contemporary society than the unsuccessful, unemployed, welfare-collecting white male.

What's *your* excuse, white boy? How can you rationalize, trivialize, or marginalize the fact that you aren't successful? It's been a white male's world in this country since it began. You've made the rules, held the highest offices, run the major corporations, and controlled the country's purse strings. Compared to your coworker counterparts, you haven't had to fight prejudice, march for civil or equal rights, petition for the right to vote, or sue for equal wages in the workplace. Your color and gender have made you more immediately acceptable, preferable, and prone to promotion for centuries.

If you are a mentally and physically healthy white male and can't find success in this country, under these most favorable conditions, you are without a doubt the biggest loser in the history of mankind. Whine all you like about affirmative action, reverse discrimination, and other injustices you see, as the balance of power begins to slowly shift away from your domain. While these corrupt practices are misguided and wrong they're not to fault for your sorry state. Your problem is that you surrendered much of the head start granted at your conception to a combination of smugness, laziness, arrogance, sloppy character, absent discipline, failure to educate yourself, and complacency—and now you've got to suck it up, swallow your pride, and get back to work before you become an irrelevant pimple in the white trash wing of the has-been hall of fame. Don't expect anyone to shed tears for you. It's high time you put down the can of Meisterbrau, get off your puke green sofa, pull up your pants over your butt cheeks, bleach the tobacco stains from your hands, brush your tooth, and get a job!

Hard-Charging Strategies

1. Become a color, gender, and ethnic-blind leader. Ditch diversity and go for results, because diversity without com-

petence is worthless. Great leaders could care less about the color of one's skin, the ethnic background of an employee, the gender of the employee, or even if the employee is confused as to his or her gender. What matters most in an elite organization is having employees with character, competence, and consistency, all which lead to positive results. Unfortunately, business leaders are a bit confused in this regard, and with good cause. Racial quotas have been ruled unconstitutional by the Supreme Court (*Bakke*, 1978, *Gratz*, 2003), but businesses and universities can nevertheless be sued if they don't have them. The hypocritical sloths in Washington, D.C. set a poor example in this arena, as 96 percent of all congressional aides on Capitol Hill are white. Go figure.

2. Redefine loyalty in your organization. Make certain everyone knows they will be measured by what they put into their time at work, not the time they put in at work. Just as you'd be tempted to judge a husband as loyal simply because he has been married to the same woman for 25 years—right up until the time you find out that he philandered for those years, and would strip him of his "loyal" moniker; so must you redefine loyalty for poorly performing long-term employees. Think about it: Bill and Hillary Clinton have been married for a lot of years, and there are many adjectives Hillary could use to describe Slick Willy, but I seriously doubt that "loyal" would be one of them.

3. Focus people on what they can control. As a leader of people you cannot let them buy into the victimhood promoted by politically correct society. Teach them

that when they choose a behavior they also choose the consequences that go with it. Preach that failure is not an accident; you either set yourself up for it or you don't. Remind your people that eighty percent of what holds them back is within their control and 20 percent is not. Even in the worst of times they can still control their attitude, discipline, character choices, work ethic, where they spend their time, and with whom they spend it. Until employees embrace the fact that it is their inside decisions and not outside conditions that determine their success they will continue to rejoice at the messengers of mercy who assure them that their sorry state in life is all someone else's fault. Somewhere along the line you must stop hiring and then keeping employees who started out in life with nothing—and decades later, still have most of it left.

4. Hold minority employees just as accountable as you would other employees. Over the years, racial instigators have fomented increasing rage against whites, blaming Caucasians for their poverty, broken families, and AIDS, to name just a few grievances. This has resulted in creating a "white guilt" and shame throughout sectors of the white race. As a result, many paleface supervisors have become afraid to confront, criticize, disagree with, correct, redirect, or fire minority employees for fear of being labeled a racist or being sued.

Issues that are performance or behavioral matters of right versus wrong have been distorted by workplace victims into matters that are black versus white. Frankly, I'm exhausted at being labeled a racist when I choose to criticize, question, or disagree with a minority. As a result, a backlash is brewing, brought on by a populace weary of being pigeonholed as bigots or racists any time they correct, hold accountable, or criticize a minority employee. Failing to hold anyone—of any color, gender, or ethnic background—accountable does a disservice to the perpetrator, betrays the rest of the team, and diminishes the organization overall.

This is why you must clearly spell out performance and behavioral expectations so that holding everyone—and I mean everyone—accountable is made easier, faster, and legally defensible.

5. Educate yourself on this topic. If you buy into one of the key premises of this book: That trends in society influence business trends, and you are alarmed at the direction you see affirmative action mindset in society and industry becoming more prominent, I recommend that you educate and arm yourself in this area so you are more aware, more capable, and more bold in your approach to combating this perverse antithesis to the merit-based psyche needed in your business. I recommend four books that are all excellent for this purpose. The first three books are written by Black American leaders concerned with the entitlement-based, "I'm a victim" mantra espoused by the problem profiteers: *Scam: How the Black Leadership Exploits Black America*, by Rev. Jesse Lee Peterson; *Creating Equal: My Fight Against Race Preferences*, by Ward Connerly; *What Color*

is a Conservative? by J. C. Watts, Jr., and *An Unlikely Conservative: The Transformation of an Ex-Liberal (Or How I Became the Most Hated Hispanic in America)*, by Linda Chavez.

CHAPTER

Don't Just Win . . . Run Up the Score!

Peering into the PC Cesspool

What happens when, in an effort to be PC, you stop playing to win and start playing not to lose in an attempt to keep the seas calm? Take a look:

1. The *Journal Star* newspaper in Lincoln, Nebraska, announced that it would no longer refer to that football team in Washington as the "Redskins," because the name is offensive. Instead, editor Kathleen Rutledge said the paper will just use the term "Washington." She has also decided to drop the stereotypical modifier, "Fighting," when used with team nicknames such as Fighting Sioux or Fighting Illini. "We have also stopped printing logos for professional and college sports teams that use Native symbols—ones that adopt imagery such as an arrowhead and ones that caricature Native Culture." Rutledge writes, "The Chief Wahoo logo of the Cleveland Indians, which we stopped using last summer, is an example of rank caricature. Instead we'll use alternative logos that stay away from Native symbols."

Letter to the Editor: I bet people can't wait to line up and read a newspaper that doesn't present things as they really are; that disguises truth, denies reality, and lies by omission. I guess being bold enough to tell it like it is asks too much of your handy-wipe of a rusepaper. By choosing to lather yourself in

PC stench you've reduced the *Journal Star* to a "rank caricature" of a real newspaper.

2. Students in Minnesota planning to perform the play *Ten Little Indians,* based on an Agatha Christie novel, were forced to change the name because it might offend Native Americans, reports the *St. Cloud Times.* Administrators at Technical High School in St. Cloud asked the students to use the title of the Christie novel, *And Then There Were None,* instead, after people involved with the American Indian outreach at St. Cloud State University complained. They said the title is based on a children's counting rhyme from the early 1900s that is derogatory. "We count objects, not people," said Principal Roger Ziemann. "The times have changed since then and we need to be more sensitive. We don't want to give the impression that we're objectifying people."

News flash for Principal Ziemann and anyone else clueless enough to utter such nonsense: Counting people does not demean them—it's a humane and legitimate practice. In fact, Principal Ziemann, how do your teachers take attendance each day in their classes? How do you think representation for congressional districts is decided—and how about the taking of a census? How do referees ensure the right number of players is on the field? It's by counting people! Leadership decisions like Principal Ziemann's prove that simply having authority doesn't make you a leader. It just gives you the chance to make a fool of yourself as you pretend to be one.

3. The Associated Press reported that officials in Malaysia pulled the plug on an ad campaign for Toyota featuring actor Brad Pitt because it was an insult to Asians. Deputy Information Minister Zainuddin Maidin said ads featuring models and personalities who don't look Asian "plant a sense of inferiority among Asians." "Why must we use their faces in our advertisements?" he asked. "Aren't our own people handsome enough?"

Dear Mr. Zainuddin: Brad Pitt makes us all look bad by comparison—not just Asians—so stop whining and get over yourself.

Business Lesson: While some aspect of your standards, business philosophy, or operating strategies may be open to interpretation or deemed as negotiable, you need to draw the line and establish certain disciplines, mindsets, and rules that steer your organization and are engraved in granite. You cannot be the king or queen of compromise and expect to earn the respect of employees or customers. You must decide to stand for something, determine what you no longer stand for, and put the good of the team ahead of disgruntled individuals who would like to reduce your vision to their comfort zone.

This isn't a license to disrespect or demean malcontents—but somewhere along the line you need to realize that when you continue to play to win and do what is right and difficult rather than what is easy and popular, you're bound to make a few waves and an enemy or two through the process. But the uncompromising mentality that powers you through this tension is the only way to sustain success, earn more than your share of the market, and build an insanely unlevel playing field slanted overwhelmingly to your advantage. In other words, you won't grow to greatness by voting, taking endless polls, surveys, and pulses to make sure everyone is smiling, happy, and in a "We Are the World" harmony.

Do You Have the Right Stuff to Win It All?

If you only want your fair share of the market and are trying to create a level playing field in your marketplace, your worthless and weak approach to leadership will render you inconsequential; it's just a matter of time. Don't get the wrong idea: You don't have to declare war on competitors or become obsessed with running them into the ground to facilitate their demise. Instead, when you shift your focus to compete more with yourself than with others, and by continually besting your own performance, you'll reap the consumption of your competitors as a happy by-product of your own quest for excellence.

Running up the score is an unnatural act in business because when you're doing well it's tempting to let up, lose your hunger, and start gormandizing the fruits of your success. Just like the football team that jumps out to a first quarter lead of 21-0, you stop throwing deep and adopt a conservative style of "play not to lose." The problem with this silliness is that you break your own momentum and let your competitors back into the game. Running up the score takes disciplined action and a steely and focused commitment from the leader. You have to push yourself hard and often. While others are resting, reflecting, and celebrating, you must attack. While they coast, you pedal harder. While they dream of the great things they want to accomplish some day, you stay awake and do them. You start earlier, finish later, and work smarter. If you're not up to these tasks, resign yourself to be just another lump of a leadership loudmouth who talks like a big dog but walks like a pissant.

Running up the score in your business takes more than big goals and hard work. It takes a disciplined and focused plan. Following are six keys to raising your organization's bar and creating a level of performance that makes building an elite organization not only feasible, but certain and sustainable.

1. Compete with Yourself More than with Others

The truest measure of your progress and success is not whether you are #1 in your field. The most telling barometer of your progress and success is whether you are better than *you* used to be. Unfortunately, you can be better than others but still be worse than you once were. And just because others are even worse than you is no reason to pound your chest in celebration. If you focus first and foremost on competing with yourself in the most relevant metrics of your business you will undoubtedly become the best in your field as well, but it will be a byproduct of your own quest for continual improvement.

2. Don't Scorn a Strong Competitor

A strong competitor is your biggest blessing. They keep you alert, urgent, and looking over your shoulder. They are the antidote to indifference and apathy that can arise toward customers when times are too easy and rosy. They prevent complacency, cause you to work harder to keep your best people, and motivate you to get out of the box in order to survive. Leaders who wish they had less competition are lazy. There's nothing wrong with working so hard on yourself that you build an elite organization that leaves your competitors crumbs to fight over. But be smart enough to realize their mere existence is a helpful catalyst to the pursuit of excellence that helped make you who are. Never wish it were easier. Always wish you were better.

3. Create a Maximization Mindset

Maximizing your business means you take steps to leverage each and every opportunity and resource at your disposal. Maximization is a mental discipline. Consistently exercising this discipline helps you bulletproof your business, makes you less susceptible to downturns, and positions you to get more than your share when business is robust. Most businesses need zero additional opportunities in order to grow. Instead, they need to become more focused on maximizing the plethora of opportunities and resources they have each day and are currently losing and abusing. Since maximizing is a mental discipline, the following 10 guidelines will help you develop the maximization mindset necessary to consistently execute.

Ten Rules for Creating a Maximization Mindset

1. Develop a daily dose of paranoia that prevents you from becoming too comfortable. A daily dose of paranoia is

like a stone in your shoe that keeps you on edge. You work each day as though someone is out to get you. You never rest, celebrate, or reflect for too long. And, most important of all, you worry. Not some panicked, neurotic type of worry; but you stay alert, remain engaged, and don't let a pat on the back turn into a massage.

2. Realize that the seeds of your next rut are often planted in the good times. It's when things are rolling along that you're most prone to get sloppy and lazy. You let up on training, holding others accountable, making necessary changes and big decisions, and start spending more time polishing a chair with your complacent rear end then staying visible, viable, and accessible in the trenches of your business.

Your abandonment of these vital disciplines doesn't show up overnight. In fact, you'd be better off if it did; if the moment you got off-track a celestial force would shout in your ear that you're getting complacent. But while a downturn in results doesn't show up overnight, it will show up over time.

Remember: When you find yourself in a rut it's not the result of something you did last night, last week, or even last month. Rather, what you're enduring is a series of failed disciplines, repeated errors in judgment, and bad decisions, sown over time, that are just now manifesting themselves. And the first rule of ruts is this: When you find yourself in a rut stop digging! In other words, stop doing the stupid things that put you there and start climbing out of the rut before it turns into a grave. The only difference between a rut and a grave is the length, depth, width, and amount of time you're in it.

3. You must create a focus and a standard to maximize every customer. This means you maximize the gross profit and that in sales organizations you gain a referral from the customer. No customer should be considered maximized until you've tried to turn one sale into two or three.

4. You should create a focus and a standard to maximize every incoming telephone sales call. Incoming sales calls are a potential gold mine for any business, but too often untrained and unprofessional employees turn the encounter into amateur hour. Answering an incoming sales call in your business should be a privilege people must earn and qualify for. It is a not a right.

5. To create a maximization mindset you should set and focus on attaining daily goals. I'm constantly stunned by the number of business professionals that do not set daily production goals for their teams. If you want to make a day mean more then put a number on it. Give your team something that creates a focus—a daily campaign, something they can celebrate if they hit and a reason for you to create urgency if they miss.

6. To create a maximization mindset, hold "Red Alert" meetings when objectives aren't met. In addition to daily goals you should have Red Alert numbers for each department in your business. For instance, from Monday to Wednesday your Red Alert production number is "ten," and from Thursday through Saturday your Red

Alert production number is "twelve." If your team misses the Monday through Wednesday number then you hold a Red Alert meeting on Thursday morning to determine why. This isn't a beat-up session. Rather, it is a chance to regroup, gain input, and correct your course before you get too far off-track.

Repeat the process if the Thursday through Saturday goal is missed. By setting these short-term objectives you compress focus and create urgency on days when there ordinarily might be very little. On the other hand, if your team hits the Red Alert numbers, reward them: a small cash bonus, or by ordering pizzas in for lunch and the like. You cannot afford to let your team get too far off-track; Red Alert objectives and meetings force you and your team to continually think about results.

7. To create a maximization mindset you must strike early each day. The best time to create momentum and focus for your team is early in the day. You should hold some type of "War Room" meeting where the key people on your staff get together to review yesterday's goal: Did you hit it or not? If not, why? What is set up for today? If it doesn't look very good, decide what you can do to breathe life into an otherwise unpromising looking day.

8. To create a maximization mindset you must leverage your current customer base. You will never grow consistently if you fail to keep the customers you already have. What are you doing to stay in contact with, incentivize, and reward your current customers? Don't fall for

the conventional trap that induces you to spend dispro-portionate percentages of your advertising budget to at-tract new customers if you've got nothing allocated to retain the customers you've already earned. You know; the folks that already like and trust and believe in you. These are the people least likely to shop your price and most likely to reward you with higher customer satis-faction scores—if you'll stay in touch with them and give them a reason to come back and do business with you. You're not doing much of anything to retain these people, you say? Then pardon my frankness, but it's time to replace the peas in your pate with brains and wake up to the fact that the cost of customer retention is miniscule when compared to the cost of client acqui-sition. You will never maximize your current opportu-nities or your resources until you are committed to leveraging the gold mine known as your current client base.

9. A maximization mindset means you invest your time and resources where you gain the highest return. As mentioned previously, some of your employees are so inept and worthless as workers that they will never amount to much. Considering this, just how much more time and resources are you willing to throw away on them as you assume the role of "savior of lost causes and chief steward of a half-way house for has-beens?"

You must get stingier with where you spend your time, money, energy, and other resources. You must become a more capable keeper of personal and corporate assets. Otherwise, you cheat the rest of your team and your company, and are unworthy of the position that gives you the latitude to be so irresponsible. You cannot afford to take a casual approach to distributing time and resources. Casualness leads to casualties.

10. A maximization culture can never be sustained unless people are held accountable for executing the disciplines you outline as nonnegotiable. Every organization needs a handful of nonnegotiable expectations that people must perform without excuse, such as: minimum performance standards; being on time, proper dress and grooming, telling the truth at all times, following up with working and sold customers, adhering to specified systems and procedures, and more.

Let me be blunt once again: If you don't have the will or resolve to maximize these 10 points you're just plain lazy. There is no other reason you'd fail to do what you know would drastically leverage your current opportunities and assets.

You will never be able to run up the score and get more than your fair share of the market for your business unless you pay attention to these 10 points. They're not the only areas that beckon for maximization, but they're a high-impact place to start.

4. Overcome Personal Complacency

When you become complacent it affects and infects the people and culture around you, because complacency, just like its opposite, urgency, is contagious. If you're in a leadership position you can't afford to become complacent, because when you let up a little, your people will let up a lot. In fact, when you catch cold your people will tend to come down with pneumonia. And don't think complacency doesn't apply to you. It applies to and affects all of us from time to time. It doesn't matter what your title, income, or net worth may be: Complacency is either a problem right now or will be in the near future.

The more successful you are the more susceptible you are to becoming complacent, because the good times tend to put you to sleep. On the other hand, it's hard to get complacent when you're failing; when you're fighting for survival and going under for the third time. At that point you're far from complacent: eyes bulging, face red, and gasping for air. Suffice it to say that if you're successful at what you do you're the most appetizing target for complacency. There's a bullet out there with your name on it and it's going to find you. Here are five tips that will help you make some waves and fight off complacency:

1. Bite off more than you can chew. If you set goals that you know for certain you can hit you're a weak stick. While it's true that goals either too high or too low cause people to mentally check out of what they're doing, your goals must be big enough to cause you to do something other than business as usual in order to achieve your ends. Your goals must force change, big decisions, risk, and a departure from your comfort zone. If your goals don't create discomfort they're impotent, because you won't grow. Thus, you should con-

sider stretch goals as a form of corporate Viagra that remedies organizational impotence.

2. Continue to upgrade your skills. It's hard to get complacent when you work as hard on yourself as you do on your job; when you learn new things that you apply and share with others and when you read a book or attend a seminar and are reminded of how much you still have to learn.

The number one obstacle to continuing to upgrade your skills is your own ego. Your ego will trick you into thinking that you're good enough; that your track record speaks for itself and that you have better things to do with your time than learn. From time to time people tell me they've lost their passion at work, and that it "just isn't fun anymore." I tell these folks to start learning again; to begin a personal growth program, because the better they get at what they do the more fun it becomes and the better they'll feel about themselves.

If you don't think you have time to upgrade personal skills you're dead wrong. Turn off the dumpster with buttons known as your television and work on you! Commit to a specific personal growth plan, such as one book or CD in your field every month, and increase your intake over time. If you learn something new and have 5 people working for you, you'll get to leverage what you learned five times. If you have 10 people working for you, you'll get a 10-multiplier benefit from what you learned. If you don't put a premium on learning you're just plain shiftless and you deserve to rot in your comfort zone as your career calcifies in a mold. And when the people around you outgrow you and pass you by you'll probably whine about how unfair the world is, but you'll know down deep who's at fault: The undisciplined, lazy lout frowning back at you in the mirror.

3. Stay physically fit. Just as working on your mind energizes you, elevates your self-esteem, and causes you to hold yourself to a higher standard, so does working on your body. It's easier to get complacent when you are an immobile, out-of-breath, out-of-shape lunk, lumbering around the workplace looking for leftover donuts. If you can't make the time to get your heart rate up for 25 minutes at least three times per week your priorities are screwed up and my bet is that your body and stamina are as well.

Make no mistake: When your mind and body become complacent they set the tone for the rest of your performance to decline at and away from work. As I explained when discussing ruts, the negative effects won't show up overnight but they *do* manifest over time. Be aware of this and get busy doing *something* to become more fit. If you can't or won't exercise, at least stop committing suicide with a fork every time you sit down to graze.

4. Associate with people who are more successful than you: financially, spiritually, with relationships, and so forth. This keeps you humble, hungry, and inspired. If you make more money than everyone you know you can become complacent. You'll spend more time comparing how well you're doing to others and use your success as a permission slip to get lazy and let up. I've got nothing against poor, unsuccessful people, but the fact is there

is little you'll learn from them. Have you ever listened to a broke bum trying to tell someone how to get rich? It's hilarious. Stop listening to people who are more screwed up than you are. As speaker Jim Rohn says, "Find out what poor people are reading and don't read those things. Find out where they're going and what they're saying and don't go there or talk like that." It's good advice.

If you don't personally know anyone more successful than you, you need to get out more—because believe me, they're out there. If you're too lax to find them then you can read about them in journals, magazines, or books. The point is not to compare yourself to them and feel inferior as a result, but to keep yourself alert to the fact that regardless of how well you're doing, you haven't yet arrived. There's still work to do.

5. Set daily goals and hold yourself accountable. Here I go with daily goals again, but the fact is there's no better way to compress your focus and make yourself do something *now*. It's tough to get complacent when you have a list of key objectives that you must achieve daily. People that set all these fancy long-term goals but then fail to set daily goals are unconsciously removing the pressure to do anything *today*.

5. Stay in an Attack Mode

Know this about human nature: The natural tendency is not to go the second mile, which is why so few people make the effort. Instead, the natural tendency—especially when you're winning—is to let up and rest a while, celebrate a while, and reflect a while. When you slide you slide backward, not forward. You need to be aware of this natural tendency, so you can set goals for yourself that help pull you through this inclination to coast. "Playing not to lose" is one of the most common errors in business and the only way to offset it is to consciously stay in an attack mode.

Following are six thoughts on staying in an attack mode: Staying in an attack mode means you continue to "fix the roof while the sun is shining" and do the following—even when things are going very well:

1. Continue to train. Training people even when they're doing well keeps them humble and lets them know there is still room to improve. In fact, when you don't train your people you send them the message that they're good enough just the way they are: a reckless and expensive message to give.

2. Hold people accountable. Even the most derelict and inept leaders can hold people accountable after the bottom falls out, but when you consistently maintain an accountability culture and apply a consistent pressure to perform you grab everyone's attention and keep them sharp, focused, and urgent.

3. Recruit, interview, and hire. This is a discipline you must execute year round, not just when your back is against the wall. The best one-word recruiting strategy is *proactive*. In fact, if you aren't consistently building a pipeline of talent you'll never have the courage to hold people accountable. You must also accept that when you

169

fail to hold someone accountable because you have no one to replace them you've chosen surrender as your corporate strategy.

4. Innovate. You cannot simply optimize your way to the next level. Innovation means you continue to devise new strategies that give you a competitive edge. Don't just focus on what makes you better, but also on what makes you different.

5. Make changes, make big decisions, and take mature risks. These things should all be done from a position of strength—when you're at the top of your game and seeing clearly, not after the stuff hits the fan.

6. Restart your momentum. Continue to lead when you hit the wall. From time to time, when visiting with a business owner or manager lamenting about how business is slow, they spew this sage advice: "It may be slow now but business will come back around. It's all about cycles." Whenever I have to indulge this nonsense from some management amateur I can't help but envy their competitors. What kind of numbskull resigns his or her business future to such a fickle fate? Of course business will eventually come around again, but if you're dumb enough to sit back and wait for it to happen you just might lose it all.

When your business hits the wall there are deliberate steps you must take to shock the culture and shift the momentum back in your favor. Author John Maxwell has said that momentum is the great exaggerator: When you have it you look better than you really are and when you lack it you look worse than you really are. So who wants to look worse than they really are for any longer than necessary? Use these steps as a blueprint to make some waves the next time your business stalls, and make something happen rather than waiting for it to happen.

Eight strategies for restarting momentum:

1. Regroup and refocus your team by selecting or redefining a target and assembling a plan to attack it. You must clearly state your objective and compress your focus by shortening the duration of the goal. In other words, forget about your quarterly forecast for a moment and zero in on a target you must reach within the next 1 to 2 weeks.

2. Set up short-term wins and celebrate each victory along the way. Take the 1- or 2-week goal and break it down to 2- or 3-day objectives. This further narrows focus and makes the objectives more real and within reach. The idea is to do all you can—pull out all stops—to hit the first of these 2- to 3-day objectives, because this is cause for celebration and a catalyst for shifting your culture. And nothing silences cynics like results: You can rest assured that these short-term wins will help bring the stragglers along.

3. Make it personal. Redefine performance expectations for each individual team member. Here's where personal accountability kicks in, because performance expectations can become cloudy or conveniently forgotten during times of crisis. After you've set the shorter-term objectives for the team overall, you've got to bring it down to a personal level by showing everyone what

their individual role is. This makes them personally accountable for doing their share and takes away the tendency to hide behind others.

4. Spend more time in the trenches so you can quickly, loudly, and publicly positively reinforce the behaviors and results you're looking for. Once you begin reinforcing people they will in turn reinforce other people; the subsequent chain reaction transforms a sleepy culture and reignites momentum. But here's the key: Once you've set the objectives you must assume the role as catalyst, by getting out of your office and into the trenches to inspire, give feedback to, and reinforce the right actions when taken by your team. In times of crisis, real leaders show up. They don't sit in their office playing solitaire on their computer or dreaming up the next excuse they'll belch out for why business is slow.

5. Redouble your efforts to focus people on what they can control. When business is slow people start pointing fingers and whipping out their black belts in blame. It's essential you coach them on how to focus on what they can control: Their attitude; their work ethic; their character choices; where they spend their time, and with whom they spend it. A victim's mindset rationalizes nonperformance and drains morale. Don't permit it!

6. If there are no customers coming through the door—or whenever a traffic count slows down considerably—set activity goals, and reward them, as they will eventually lead to results.

I consulted with an automotive dealership during the infamous sniper attacks in the nation's capital: There was no way to get customers to leave their homes and come in to wander around the vulnerable, wide-open spaces of a car dealership. Thus, we focused each salesperson on making "x" number of calls to their customer base to ask for referrals; set appointments for the following week, and check on their overall satisfaction. These activities not only created future sales but also kept people busy and focused on productive actions, and took their minds and conversations off the crisis that surrounded them.

Even in the worst of times people want to feel that they're doing *something* productive. Besides, it's tough to be inspired when you're either bored, distracted, or depressed.

7. Develop yourself in the down times. When business turns south, redouble your efforts to develop yourself mentally, physically, and spiritually during the down times. This sure beats the alternative of drinking, eating, and smoking yourself into oblivion to escape the daily pressures the crisis has wrought. It also helps you maintain your personal passion and momentum, and will go a long way in inspiring your team. After all, the speed of the leader is the speed of the pack.

8. Don't let up on accountability during tough times. Even if it's more difficult to hold people accountable for tangible results, you should hold them accountable for executing prescribed activities. Otherwise, bad habits and an air of lethargy takes root, which will further weaken your culture and prolong the crisis.

Hard-Charging Strategies

1. Focus on being your best. If you're not better than you used to be nothing else matters much, because you're on your way to down and then out.

2. Stop whining about not having enough opportunities and start maximizing the opportunities and resources you're abusing every day. You don't need more opportunities to grow: You need to better leverage those you already have.

3. If you want to run up the score in your business and earn more than your fair share of the marketplace while others rest, reflect, relax, or reel you must attack.

4. Remember that since staying in an attack mode is an unnatural act you will have to deliberately pull yourself and your team through the natural tendency to let up.

5. Fighting off team complacency begins with you fighting off personal complacency. As a leader, you simply can't afford to have many bad days.

6. Keep working on yourself, because regardless of how good you think you are, you're not good enough. The day you think you are is the day you begin to decline.

7. Don't make excuses. Before you can stop accepting excuses from others you must stop making them. Excuses are wonderful, aren't they? They absolve you of responsibility; they comfort you in immobility and they insulate you from reality, all the while permitting you to dig your next rut with your mouth. When your people hear you making excuses you give them license to do likewise exponentially. Suck it up and bear it. Take responsibility

even when it's hard: Work through immobility even when it hurts, and face reality even when it's hideous.

8. Don't accept excuses. If you don't make them you've earned the right not to accept them. Focus others on controllables.

9. Hold people accountable. Nothing protects and sustains a high performance culture quite like a positive pressure to perform.

10. Never wait for momentum to come back around. Use the steps listed to jumpstart it. And when you do have momentum, remember that rest should be a necessity and not an objective. Never, ever, break your own momentum. It's one of the most dastardly leadership sins.

11. Remember the warning at the beginning of this chapter: If you are committed to building an elite organization you cannot afford to play not to lose, keep the seas calm and the course slow and steady. You must get your game face on: Play to win, and when you're winning, run up the score! Anything less is shameless underachievement.

CHAPTER

Spare the Rod, Spoil the Sluggard!

Peering into the PC Cesspool

When there are no consequences for wrong actions, the wrong actions will continue. In an age when political correctness has made us afraid to hold others accountable for the results of their actions you don't have to look far to see the impact of this trend. In business it affects the bottom line. In society it can lead to death and destruction. See for yourself:

Action: February, 1993, the World Trade Center is bombed by terrorists, killing five and injuring hundreds.
Consequence: The United States did nothing.

Action: October, 1993, 18 American troops are killed in a firefight in Somalia by thugs made up of and supported by terrorists.
Consequence: President Clinton orders a retreat and has the troops brought home. Osama bin Laden later told ABC News, "The youth . . . realized more than before that the American solider was a paper tiger and after a few blows ran in defeat."

Action: November, 1995, five Americans are killed and 30 are wounded by a car bombing in Saudi Arabia by terrorists.
Consequence: The United States did nothing.

Action: June, 1996, a U.S. Air Force housing complex in Saudi Arabia is bombed by terrorists.
Consequence: The United States did nothing.

Action: Months later, Saddam Hussein attacked the Kurdish-controlled city of Erbil.

Consequence: President Clinton had missiles fired into Iraq, hundreds of miles from Saddam's forces.

Action: November, 1997, Iraq refused to allow U.N. weapons inspectors to do their jobs and threatened to shoot down a U.S. U-2 spy plane.

Consequence: February, 1998, President Clinton threatened to bomb Iraq but called it off when the U.N. said no.

Action: August 7, 1998, U.S. embassies in Kenya and Tanzania are bombed by terrorists, killing 224 and injuring 5,000.

Consequence: The United States did nothing.

Action: August 20, 1998, Monica Lewinsky appeared for the second time to testify before a grand jury.

Consequence: President Clinton created a diversion to this testimony by bombing Afghanistan and Sudan, damaging three camels and an aspirin factory.

Action: October, 2000, the warship USS *Cole* was attacked by terrorists, killing 17 and injuring dozens.

Consequence: The United States did nothing.

Action: All listed acts of terror documented herein, and the escalating threat to our national security, occurred during Bill Clinton's presidency.

Consequence: President Clinton reduced the active duty military force from 2.1 million to 1.6 million men and women; reduced the army from 18 full-strength light and mechanized divisions to 12, reduced naval warships from 546 to 380, toward a targeted force of 300—the smallest naval force since the pre-World War II period, and shrunk the Air Force from 76 flight squadrons down to 50.[1]

Action: September 11, 2001.

Business Lesson: Behavioral science teaches that if you want to change a behavior you must change the consequence for that behavior. Whether dealing with international terrorists or your own brand of corporate terrorists, who come in late, violate your values, fail to hit prescribed objectives, and otherwise don't do what you're paying them to do, until you change the consequence and hold them accountable for their misdeeds you can expect to see more of it. In fact, by failing to impose a consequence, you unwittingly endorse their behavior and ask for more trouble.

If employees come in late to work, they may continue coming in late until there's a consequence for doing so—and it's your fault, because they're just doing what works; if they lie to customers they'll continue to do so until there's a consequence for their dishonesty, and if they continue to fall short of the required production levels but suffer no consequences for their failure, you sanction their mediocrity by failing to crack the whip of consequences. Learn how to leverage consequences or you'll become a doormat for every malcontent, thief, liar, troublemaker, and nonperformer in your organization. As Dr. Phil says, "You teach people how to treat you." And consequences are your #1 instruction manual. In simplest terms, consequences are the "or else" and far too many leaders today have forgotten those two words.

You Teach People How to Treat You

However your employees treat you or behave on a regular basis is the result of consequences: effective, impotent, or non-existent, that you've applied in the past. In fact, you see this principle in effect everywhere: at home, for instance. If your kids are rotten, spoiled brats, you created that mess by reinforcing their deficient behavior with big talk but empty threats. And now you're reaping the consequences. Unfortunately, the rest of us have to reap the consequences as well, whenever we encounter your little critters in public: screaming at the table next to ours in the restaurant, running down the aisle of the airplane, and blabbing their loud mouths at the movies. In fact, if you have bratty kids—and you know who you are—do us all a favor when you go on your next vacation and drive, don't fly. The rest of us don't want to hear, see, or smell your beasts on any airliner we're on. Travel is stressful enough without feeling like we're in a zoo. I wish the airlines would create a policy to keep bratty kids out of first class, preferably seating them in the baggage compartment with popcorn and video games, out of sight, hearing, and mind. Every business traveler I know would line up to fly on a brat-free airline. We've banned smoking on flights, why not brats?

Now don't jump to conclusions. I don't dislike kids. In fact, I have a daughter and nephews I love and respect immensely, and know many friends with well-mannered and courteous offspring. Kids—regardless of their behavior—are a reflection of either deficit parenting or well-honed parenting skills, just as the people on your team are a direct re-

181

flection of your deficit leadership or well-developed skills. The same principle applies.

The Need for Discipline

In today's politically correct cesspool, discipline has become a bad word. Teachers can't even discipline kids that get out of line any more. What a shame, because people develop to their potential in structured environments; where there are clear expectations, intense instruction and accountability for results. One or two swats and you'll be surprised how quick a kid will turn around. I'm speaking from experience. In fifth grade music class I once got ticked off at a classmate and threw a drumstick that hit his head. Right after class the teacher told me to stay put, went and got another teacher as a witness and gave me four loud swats with a paddle. They didn't need to call my parents to ask permission and they didn't have their hands cuffed by sissified liberal laws. I messed up and got what I deserved. And you know what else? I never, ever, caused a problem in class again—until the eighth grade, when, while attending school in Canada, I punched a kid during history class for booing the American flag when it was shown on the slide projector during a presentation on the War of 1812. But hey, three years of model behavior was a great outcome from the four swats in the fifth grade.

Discipline is a key success ingredient—and it's missing from too many lives today. First, there is little discipline to pay the price for success and secondly, discipline isn't imposed as a consequence for failed performances. Why are so many people fat today? It's not ignorance. People know what makes

182

them fat. It's a lack of discipline. Why do only 10 percent of readers make it past the first chapter in a book they spend money to buy? Lack of discipline. Why do so many people spend their lives jumping from one job to another? Lack of discipline to stay put and pay the price for success. When they don't get rich quick they're off looking for an easier way. They spend their entire lives looking for ways to avoid pain and discomfort, instead of working through it and building the necessary character and competence to make it big.

Here are three key thoughts on discipline that will make waves in your own life and help you become a better person and leader.

1. Become more disciplined in how you spend your time. Narrow your focus. Give up the trivial so you can spend more time with the ultimate. Remember, you can do 40 things every day and leave a blur or 4 things well and leave a mark. Schedule as much of your day in advance as possible because unmanaged time will normally flow to wasteful things, surrender to every emergency, and come under the influence of the dominant people in your life.

2. Become more disciplined with whom you spend your time with. The Bible warns that evil company corrupts good habits.[2] It also says that he who walks with the wise will be wise but the companion of fools will be destroyed.[3]

3. Realize that discipline is a morale-builder. You feel better about yourself when you're structured and accountable, when you deny yourself certain things and spend time doing the right tasks.

The Need for Accountability

I've written at length about accountability throughout this book. And there's a reason: It is essential to tightening up, toughening up, and leading more effectively in today's too tolerant times. Holding your people accountable for results creates urgency, focus, and a positive pressure to perform. Leaders reluctant to hold others accountable for performance are like tonsils: they're worthless so you may as well remove them:

Creating a strong accountability culture does more to define your workplace environment than your eight-inch-thick procedure manual, impassioned speeches about delivering results, and countless pep talks combined. When people are held accountable they cannot simply go through the motions and mark time doing unacceptable amounts of work, reading the paper, smoking, joking, or spitting in a cup as they lounge around the workplace hoping not to be noticed, at least not for long. There are three key components to holding others accountable that you must put in place to keep your people focused on results.

1. Define clear expectations, including minimum performance standards, and attach appropriate consequences.

Since ambiguity is the enemy of accountability expectations must be clear and easy to measure. Good people will try hard to hit a standard if they know what it is, but it's difficult for them to work longer and harder if where they're headed is obscured by fog. As Vince Lombardi said, "It's hard to be aggressive when you're confused." When you create a vague performance standard, such as "We expect you to work hard," you guarantee cloudy and convenient interpretations. On the other hand: "In any 90-day period, you must average at least eight sales per month or you can no longer work here" leaves no gray area. Notice that this definition of an expectation includes a clear consequence: "you can no longer work here."

Expectations without clear consequences are impotent and are reduced to mere suggestions. Some propose that such cut-and-dried guidelines don't leave enough room for individual customization. But by establishing minimum standards for accountability you are actually declaring a benchmark for performance, under which you are unwilling to compromise. If you don't create these parameters and deliberately choose to stand for something specific, you stand for nothing by default, and will find numerous and creative ways to excuse, rationalize, and trivialize poor performance, and attribute it to someone's "unique situation."

If you fail to create performance clarity you will be reluctant to hold others accountable, because you know, down deep, that you never specifically established what must be done, so you will hesitate to confront deficient outcomes. After all, how can you say to me, "Anderson, you're not cutting it?" if you've never defined what "cutting it" is? You can't. So you won't. Thus, poor performance will continue unchecked, and will wreak havoc on your organization's standards, morale, momentum, and credibility.

Your people deserve to know where they stand and where you stand. Clear expectations and consequences take the guesswork out of what is or isn't acceptable. Always set expectations at minimum expected levels of performance and as a negative guarantee, because you don't want someone to reach the objective and then hit the snooze button and coast. A negative guarantee means that just because you hit the prescribed standard doesn't mean you automatically keep your job. Factors like attendance, character, team play, and customer care must also be considered. On the other hand, a negative guarantee establishes that if an employee doesn't hit the expectation, he or she will suffer the consequence. Obviously, the consequence doesn't have to be termination. It can be anything from probation, loss of certain pay incentives, or other privileges.

Whatever you choose should be clear and concise, and make sure you can live with it and follow through. Because the first time you fail to enforce a pre-prescribed consequence you render it worthless: Your credibility will be impaired as your people mock you behind your back. "Don't worry about those expectations because the boss won't follow through. He talks like John Wayne but walks like Woody Allen."

Ideally, you will establish both performance and behavioral expectations as discussed in Chapter 1. Behavioral expectations are often referred to as core values. These are behaviors that make up the DNA of your organization, and for which you've determined you are unwilling to compromise on. If you don't establish expectations and hold others accountable for both performance and behavioral standards you will either wind up with nice folks with great values who can't or won't get the job done, or skunks that do.

2. Provide the tools they need to execute.

As a leader, you have every right to establish clear and high performance expectations, but you cannot do so credibly until you have provided the support to get the job done: training, fast and direct feedback on performance, and the personal coaching that the employee needs to reach the goal. Many leaders decide to raise the bar in their business and begin demanding more from their people, but don't provide the tools to succeed. This is leadership betrayal. If all your people have ever done is run around the block, and you're going to ask them to run a marathon, you're obliged to do your part and get them ready. There is little more frustrating to an employee than wanting to do a good job and knowing what needs to be done but lacking the tools, training, and support needed to execute.

A key element of support that you must provide to each employee is our old friend, feedback. Feedback must be given informally, on the fly, throughout the day, as well as formally at reviews. If you are serious about holding people accountable and keeping them focused on consistent results then you must accept the fact that no news is not good news and deliver the feedback your people need to succeed and grow.

3. Get out of their way.

After you clearly define expected outcomes and necessary consequences, establish timelines and provide the tools to succeed—don't micromanage the process. Make yourself available for support, then get out of your employees' way and let them run. I've seen too many good people leave organizations because they weren't allowed to make decisions, think, act, or initiate on their own. You sure can't blame them. After all, who wants to work with a boss so foolish as to invest in the growth of his or her employees and then prevent them from using their new skills? In fact, if you're going to train your people and then not allow them to use what they've been taught, they're worse off than they were before training, because of the helplessness and frustration that comes with knowing what to do but not being able to do it.

Accountability is not a bad word. Too many leaders are apologetic when it comes to expecting people to do the job they're being paid to perform, or heaven forbid, actually stretch to a second-mile effort. Accountability keeps everyone sharp and provides clarity for expected results. Accountability moves your people out of a gray area and into the realm of the absolutes, where there is winning and losing, success and failure, right and wrong. Consistent results without accountability is mostly luck and is never sustainable. But the key to accountability is to couple it with the necessary components. You cannot hold people accountable for missing the mark if you fail to define the target, don't equip them for the trip, or meddle with and nitpick them throughout the process.

Two Examples of how to leverage consequences:

1. Coach John Wooden

In a prior chapter I explained how UCLA men's basketball coach John Wooden made waves to win 10 national titles. He didn't achieve that apex by being afraid of leveraging consequences, even with his best players. In the book, *Wooden: A Lifetime of Observations and Reflections On and Off the Court* (Contemporary Books, 1997), Wooden tells the story of his team and him returning from a 10-day break to find star player Bill Walton sporting a beard, which was against UCLA regulations. Wooden asked if Walton had forgotten something, to which Walton mentioned that he believed very strongly in his right to wear his beard and should be allowed to keep it. Wooden looked at him and said politely, "Bill, I have a great respect for individuals who stand up for those things in which they believe. I really do. And the team is going to miss you."[4]

Walton then went to the locker room to shave the beard before practice began, and no one was angry or harbored ill feelings. Walton knew his coach well enough to understand that he didn't bluff; that when he said something he meant it and would follow through.

This is truly the essence of effective accountability: no name-calling, no thrown objects, raised voices, or public tantrums. Instead, clearly set expectations, caring enough about people to confront them humanely and professionally, and a reputation for doing what you say you'll do goes further than bullying, threatening, or personal attacks against the employee.

2. President Ronald Reagan

One of the advantages of living in Southern California is that I'm just minutes away from the Ronald Reagan Presidential Library in Simi Valley. If you make it out this way, plan to visit this facility. It is world class, and walking in the shadow of Reagan can't help but heighten your leadership I.Q.

On August 3, 1981, the executive board of the Professional Air Traffic Controllers Organization (PATCO) rejected a proposed agreement, and over 70 percent of the FAA's 17,000 air traffic controllers went on strike.[5] The strike presented a vexing dilemma for the new president, as (1) PATCO was one of the few unions to endorse Reagan for President, (2) Reagan had a union background, as he was the first president who was a lifetime member of the AFL-CIO, was president of the Screen Actor's Guild for 6 terms, and led its first strike, and (3) Reagan agreed that the controllers deserved more money. What he didn't agree with was that they were breaking their signed covenant not to strike against the public safety. He went on television to read verbatim the agreements they were breaking and gave them 48 hours to return to work or otherwise be fired—and then he followed through with the firings. An expert on the Soviet Union later stated that, "The way the PATCO strike was handled impressed the Russians . . . and gave them respect for Reagan. It showed them a man who, when aroused, will go to the limit to back up his principles."

Reagan's decision was neither easy nor convenient. But from that point on, friend and foe alike knew Reagan was for real and to doubt his resolve and principles at their own peril.

Hard-Charging Strategies

1. At the risk of driving you nuts with my nagging, I feel obliged to remind you again that without clear expectations you don't have the benchmark or credibility to hold people accountable and apply consequences for their derelict actions. If you still don't have clearly de-

fined performance and behavioral expectations you just don't get it. I discussed this at length back in Chapter 2. Get busy, and do your job!

2. Consequences should be spelled out in advance and should be specific. Simply saying, "If you do this again you'll be in big trouble" is worthless. What does "big trouble" mean? I haven't heard that since I was 6 years old. Does it mean I'll have to stand in a corner or get a spanking? For some employees, the latter consequence would be more of a reinforcer than a detriment.

3. Consequences are in the eyes of the receiver. Getting mad at someone and sending him or her home for the day might be exactly what they're hoping for. Make certain that what you intend as a consequence serves the purpose you desire.

4. Deliver consequences as quickly after the action as possible. Delayed consequences lose their punch. Get there fast. Let them know that you're paying attention and that you mean business.

5. Consequences are intended for one purpose: to improve performance. They are not designed to demean or humiliate.

6. Realize that when you don't employ consequences on someone that deserves them you secretly begin to resent the person. This eats up your insides and further erodes your relationship with the person.

7. Don't hold a grudge. After the consequences are delivered get back to business. Nursing a grudge will diminish you far more than the person you resent.

8. Follow-through. If you don't follow through with a threatened consequence your credibility will disappear. Follow through: even when it's expensive, inconvenient, unpopular, and just plain painful. Temporary discomfort is better than temporary ease if it averts permanent failure.

CHAPTER 9

Don't Make People Happy. . . . Make Them Better!

Peering into the PC Cesspool

I suggest you read the next few paragraphs sitting down. I only have the heart to inflict on you three examples of how political correctness, in its attempt to make everyone happy, panders to oddballs, whiners, and victims. But three seems like quite enough.

1. According to the *Rocky Mountain News* a December parade in Denver will feature everyone from Chinese lion dancers to gay and lesbian shamans—but not Christians who want to sing yuletide hymns or carry a Merry Christmas message.

2. Tommy Craft, principal of Cedar Shoals High School in Athens, Georgia, apologized for reading a poem called "The New School Prayer" over the school's intercom. It was a satirical ditty about how kids today can elect pregnant prom queens and dress like freaks but can't mention God in school. Principal Craft said he just wanted to provoke a little thought. But because the poem sounded like a prayer and mentioned God, some parents complained. "Basically, I found the poem offensive, but even if I didn't, I still would believe it crossed the line between church and state," said Ginger Smith, whose daughter is a junior at Cedar Shoals.

3. *The Sarasota Herald Tribune* says some schools in Florida are so worked up over the thought of anything smacking

of Christianity appearing in classes that they are banning seasonal celebrations altogether. In this year's winter concert at Freedom Elementary School in East Manatee students will be celebrating patriotism instead of Christmas and the holidays. Even snowflakes are outlawed among the classroom decorations. "There's a lot of rules and regulations out there," said Freedom Principal Gary Holbrook. "You're trying to be respectful of everyone."

How much longer are the leaders in our government, schools, and other institutions going to worry about making everyone happy? How long will they diminish what is right for what is convenient? Because a time is coming when a moral majority of people will say that enough is enough. They'll stop sending their kids to public schools; boycott the Hollywood filth disguised as film; turn off their "do whatever makes you feel good" television programs; switch to an intelligent, unbiased newscaster; cancel their subscriptions to dishonest newspapers and periodicals; fire immoral politicians, and show less tolerance for society's whiners and losers intent on demanding from productive society what they can't earn on their own.

Business Lesson: The same mousy mindset that chooses what's convenient over what is right will cause you to lower the bar and weaken the strong in order to strengthen the weak in your organization. The business lesson here is simple: Understand that your job is not to make everyone happy. Not only is this impossible: It is unimportant. Instead, your job is to get people better, and if getting people better doesn't make them happier then get rid of them, because you have the wrong people.

What the World Needs Now Is a Little Less Tolerance

Calm down. I'm not referring to religious or ethnic intolerance. After all, I've said enough in this chapter about persecuted Christians. I'm speaking of becoming more intolerant of the people that can't cut it in your organization because they don't live your values or can't hit your numbers. You know who I mean: the charter members of the warehouse for wimps in your enterprise, many who exhibit the same killer instinct as Barney. If you let society's trend influence your business thinking today you'll sell out the productive to pacify the pathetic. Here are five politically incorrect strategies for getting people better instead of wasting your time trying to make them happy.

1. Run your business more like a team than a family. Think of how you rationalize the derelict members of your immediate or extended family: *"I know Uncle Fred can't keep a job but he is family," "Sure, Edna and her whole brood are white trash, but we have to invite them to the wedding," "Of course, he's going to ask to borrow money when he gets here, but he's my brother, what am I supposed to do?"* If you are one of the few that has no oddball, megaflop family members to help reinforce this point, then remember Cousin Eddie from the Chevy Chase movie, *Christmas*

Vacation. He was the broke loser who hadn't had a job in 7 years (he was holding out for management) and unexpectedly brought his inbred-looking brood to Clark Griswold's house at Christmas time to mooch, borrow, and eat them out of house and home. And of course the Griswold clan put up with it because stupid, lazy, white trash Cousin Eddie was "family."

I'm not knocking the tolerance and support of deadbeat family members. It's natural and sometimes necessary. But when you start to think and act in this "family model" mindset at work it can destroy the fiber of your enterprise.

Family models are too forgiving, too tolerant, and too inclusive to work well in a high-performance business culture. On the other hand, members of a team must prove themselves over again each day; there is pressure to perform; all members are held accountable, and nonperformers find themselves off the team.

2. Set minimum standards and fire those that can't make the grade. In case you thought I was finished harassing you about the importance of these standards, think again. In fact, have you established these standards yet? If not, why? As a leader, somewhere along the line you've got to decide below which performance level you are no longer willing to compromise on. Set and establish these minimum performance standards, communicate them before hiring, put them in writing, and hold people accountable for reaching them. Remember, your standards may be something like: "If you can't av-

erage eight unit sales per month for a consecutive 90-day period you are on probation. If it happens again in a 12-month period you can't work here anymore. It doesn't mean you're a bad person; you're just a bad fit. We still love you. Just go bring down sales someplace else. Don't go away mad. Just go away."

With these standards you give people a clear focus on what they must do to remain employed; you have taken away the excuse of ignorance ("I didn't know that's what you expected," etc.) and you have created a benchmark for future accountability. You've also ensured that you're not tempted to keep nonperformers too long, because those who can't cut it wind up firing themselves. You can start the standards at one point and raise them over time. If at this stage in the book you still aren't convinced these standards would help strengthen your culture, stop the wrong people hanging around too long, separate the victors from the victims, and send the appropriate message of support to your top people, you're running out of time to do what's right—so get moving! Haven't you done what is easy and convenient long enough?

3. Hold managers more personally responsible for the development of their people. There's no greater way to measure a manager than by whether the people working for him or her improve. A manager's people are his or her scorecard, and bonuses should be tied to the measurable improvement of the people working for him or her. No improvement, no bonuses. Big improvement, big bonuses. It doesn't get any fairer than that. And if a manager has such a high degree of employee turnover

in the workforce that you can't measure the improvement of his or her people, the next person to leave the organization needs to be that manager. And speaking of firing bad managers, let's go to the next point.

4. Fire bad managers faster. You should give bad managers less time, fewer chances, and a shorter rope for getting the job done, because bad managers compound the misery in an organization more quickly and completely than any other factor. Until you become less tolerant of bad managers your organization doesn't have a prayer of reaching its potential. Set clear expectations; give them the training, coaching and feedback they need to succeed, and hold them accountable for results. If they can't cut it from there, dump them.

Incidentally, you shouldn't have to spend excessive time trying to motivate your managers. The best workers are self-motivated and bring drive and desire to the table. If you find yourself having to continually pump up one of your leaders, give him or her pep talks and coddle his or her feelings, it indicates that you've made a hiring error and that you should free him or her up to find a future at something for which he or she's more suited.

5. Empower according to ability and micromanage when necessary. Empowerment is one of the most overused words in business over the past 2 decades: When I hear someone utter the word I reach for Maalox.

Yes, empowerment is important, but not everyone in your business deserves the same level of empowerment. And if you've made the mistake of hiring morons you can forget empowerment altogether and change your strategy to micromanagement. While micromanagement is a poor plan for developing people, it's the only way your business will survive when littered with losers. On the other hand, micromanage your great people and you will lose them. Don't get overinvolved and create complexity where it doesn't belong. Don't nitpick, second-guess, or tie the hands of your best people. You need them more than they need you, and don't you ever forget it.

"Warm and Fuzzy" Has Run Its Course

While the command and control, do it my way or the highway, don't get out of that box, and "if I want your opinion I'll give it to you" style of management is as inane today as it was 25 years ago, you can't get away with it now like you did back then. This is the age of the free agent, and people are much more willing to change jobs, and to do so more often. On the other hand, filling your employee's ears with choruses of happy hot-tub talk isn't the answer, either. When the loud sucking sound heard at work is your own lips unlocking from your employee's bottom, you've gone too far in the warm and fuzzy direction.

Quite frankly, many leaders need to stop singing "Kumbaya" and get tough with their people again. Business has gotten too soft. We're reluctant to offend people who need to hear the truth; they need to have their feelings hurt and get shaken out of denial, because they're not only failing, they're becoming outright failures. Your people need to worry about keeping you happy. After all, they're not volunteers; you're paying them for their services. This doesn't mean you should become disrespectful, demeaning, or abusive to people. In fact, it's quite the contrary. The greatest respect you can show them is by setting expectations that stretch them; giving feedback that is honest; caring enough to confront them when they're off-track; and holding them accountable and relentlessly training them to improve their skills.

Hard-Charging Strategies

1. Abandon excessive tolerance of underperformers. If someone is making what you define as measurable progress in reasonable time, keep working with him or her. Even if they are slower getting started than you'd like, the fact that they are making steady upward movement makes them ideal candidates for development. However, when people hover at or below average performance levels, with no sign of an upward trend, you should lose interest in continuing your relationship and sever your losses.

2. Tell the truth. One of the recurring themes of this book is to be an honest and direct leader. Care enough to confront them; give timely, honest feedback, and keep them out of a gray area.

3. Don't be disrespectful. Being direct doesn't mean you are rude or demeaning. Love the performer, hate the performance. Don't get personal. Only authors are al-

lowed to do so, in order to support certain points and put deserving dunces in their place.

4. Ask questions, seek feedback, listen closely, but don't vote. Business is neither a democracy nor a dictatorship. The most effective enterprises are normally a mix of both, but in this age, if you favor one over the other you're well advised to slightly favor the dictatorial side. If the decision is yours to make, then make it. And do so without regard to making people happy, but with absolute regard for making them better.

CHAPTER 10

Don't Trade Your Values for Valuables!

Peering into the PC Cesspool

For several years my business articles have appeared in over 100 publications annually. In addition, I write a monthly leadership column for *Dealer* magazine, which is read by tens of thousands of leaders in the 22,000 retail automotive dealerships in America. In a December article I decided to go out of my way to wish my readers a "Merry Christmas." I didn't use the term "Happy Holidays," or "Have a Nice Winter Break." As a Christian, I have always said, "Merry Christmas," because, and correct me if I'm wrong, December 25th was set aside to celebrate the birth of Jesus Christ. While the overall response from my readers was uplifting and positive, I can't say I was surprised shortly after the column appeared to receive the following message from an offended reader and ex-customer.

> *Dave Anderson,*
>
> *I'm writing to say that I am very disappointed. I have attended your seminars, bought your products, and used your web site. However, last night, I read your article in* Dealer *magazine. I feel that your interest in the past few years in being "not politically correct" has more often seemed to me as an effort at being controversial, and less an effort at doing your job better. Until last night, I just disregarded your politics and remained focused on what you could teach me to improve myself in my business. Last night, though, I read your passage where you refused to say Happy Holidays, instead stating a*

Merry Christmas and that Jesus is the "reason for the season." Well, he may be the reason for your season, but as a Jew, he is not the reason for mine. Therefore, based upon your comment that I am not to be wished a happy holiday season because I am not a Christian, I will take that as a statement that I should also not continue to support your business interests. Good luck without me, and Happy Holidays.

Name withheld by the author to protect the offended party's privacy

My reply to my former customer read as follows:

Dear "Reader,"

First, thank you for your kind wishes for a Happy Holiday and for reading Dealer *magazine. I'm sorry to hear that my kind Christmas greetings disappointed you. In response to your e-mail, please consider the following:*

The politically incorrect writing and speaking you mention in your message reflects who I am and how I think. I don't intend to tiptoe around issues in an effort to not offend others. Never have; never will. There's far too much of this going on today in society and business, and it's debilitating to high-performance cultures. Pointing out how political correctness in society influences how you run your business does help me do my job better. Telling people what I believe they need to hear instead of what they want to hear also helps me do my job better. And if you choose to interpret my bluntness, disregard for being politically correct, and saying what's on my mind as an effort to try and become controversial, that is your privilege.

If you have a problem with my style or my content, you certainly did the right thing by terminating the relationship

205

you had with my company. We appreciate all customers and hate to lose any of them, but I decided long ago to never trade my values for valuables. And while I always welcome comments from readers I don't appreciate attempts at censorship.

    I also suggest you reread my Christmas greeting to my readers. It did not say, as you mention in your e-mail, that "Jesus is the reason for the season." This is a misquote. Rather, it said, "Don't let the politically correct nonsense in society dull your senses to the real reason for the Christmas season." Mr. Reader, regardless of your religion, Jesus is the real reason for the Christmas season. Period. While other holidays are celebrated during this time of year, what I said is 100 percent accurate in that the only reason we celebrate Christmas itself— I specifically mention December 25th in my greeting—is because of the birth of Jesus Christ. And as a Christian, this is how I choose to greet people and wish them well. Frankly, if saying, "Merry Christmas" offends people it is their problem, not mine. When my grocer wished me a Happy Hanukkah yesterday I accepted his kind greetings and believed the best in his intentions rather than the worst. I didn't feel disappointed or excluded—simply grateful for his considerate thoughts.

    Incidentally, if you expect others to display tolerance and sensitivity toward your beliefs, shouldn't you do the same? Your failure to do so is a bit hypocritical, don't you think? I'll make you a deal: Let's both give out holiday greetings in the manner we see fit, with the understanding that how we choose to do so is none of the others' business. Fair enough?

Dave Anderson

Business Lesson: How far should you go to please a customer? Answer: As far as you have to, within reason. Sadly, it is sometimes necessary to fire customers. In my company, when a customer abuses our employees, we fire that customer. If a customer insists that I remove Christ from my Christmas greeting in order to make him or her happy or keep his or her business, he or she asks too much, and we must not pursue or apologize to, but fire that customer, because we won't trade our values for valuables, and neither should you. In fact, rather than hide or compromise your values, you should use your company as a platform to promote them. Believe me: This takes guts, and is easier said than done. But I'm counting on you to do what is right and not what's merely convenient.

The Toughest Strategy of All

This final hard-charging strategy will take the most courage and make the biggest waves of all. You may not have the heart or guts for this now, but some day your conscience will tell you that you've procrastinated long enough and that in addition to making money, it's time to start making a difference. After all, business should be more than a profit vehicle; it should provide a platform to make the world a better place. And rather than being passive little patsies who surrender their values to politicians and militant social outcasts who protest and picket for sport, business leaders should become activists for causes they believe make the world in which they do business a more productive planet. Sometimes this is scary, since advocating certain social or political views oftentimes alienates customers and costs you money. So rather than do what you believe is right, political correctness may silence you into immobility, and you'll be tempted to trade your values for valuables. Don't do it!

Personally, I know the rewards and penalties of what I promote in this chapter firsthand, since I have followed my own advice for years. My company champions and funds causes that range from the smuggling of Bibles into communist countries to the training of Christian leaders in hostile parts of the world to supporting political figures who share and promote our values. And as I wouldn't suggest you do something I haven't done in my own business, and since I believe in leading by example, I'll include instances of how my company, LearnToLead, has made the commitment to make the world in which we and our customers live and do business better than we found it. We're certainly not alone in doing so. Companies like Ben & Jerry's and The Body Shop have used their status and fortune to champion causes they believe in for years. You needn't agree with the causes we or other companies promote, and I don't list them here to try and enlist your support. Rather, I want to give a real-life blueprint of how to implement this tenth strategy and to encourage you to get involved with meaningful efforts that reflect your values and that will leave a legacy.

What Championing a Cause Doesn't Mean

Championing a cause doesn't mean you simply write a check to your local United Way chapter. It's not that simple. Championing a cause means you get personally as well as financially involved and that you use your name, your personal prestige, and your business as a vehicle to visibly promote the cause. Following are three articles posted in the God & Country section of our web site, www.learntolead.com. This site has thousands of subscribers who read the free training articles posted. We provide these articles free of charge and add new articles several times per year. This is one way we give back to our customers as well as to people around the world whom we'll never meet and who will never spend a cent with us.

While www.learntolead.com features articles on sales, management, and leadership, God & Country is dedicated to causes we want to promote and encourage others to support. It is the website's newest section and it has been the most controversial—as well as the most rewarding. Its funny how those two often go hand in hand in life, isn't it? The God & Country articles are designed to educate, create awareness, and inspire action.

While it is unconventional to mix views on politics and religion with business (and it isn't necessary that you go as far as we do in this regard), the positive feedback we receive, the goodwill we build, and the impact we've made has been profound. Besides, I want our clients and potential clients to know where we stand. I don't want them doing business with us under false pretenses. The result? When I look in the mirror I don't have to wince, and when I lay down to sleep I'm out like a light.

Example 1

Will You Cease Praying or Pray without Ceasing was written to highlight just how far intolerance has swung against people of faith and to underscore the problem of allowing a minority of whiners to dictate the values of a majority.

God & Country
Will You Cease Praying or Pray without Ceasing?

The Bible instructs us to pray without ceasing but the courts have trumped God to insist that we cease praying: at school; prior to sporting events; at military commencements; and publicly in general.

In a twist of the Constitution's original intent, activists use a phrase not even found in the Constitution, "separation of church and state" to justify banning God. I wonder if these people have ever read the First Amendment, because its meaning is the opposite of what they claim. The First Amendment states that "Congress shall make no law restricting an establishment of religion or prohibiting the free expression thereof." Somehow the ACLU, atheists, and droves of clueless leftists miss the last six words: "or prohibiting the free expression thereof."

If a majority of Americans are Christians—and they are—and they wish to engage in a 30-second prayer prior to a football game to ask God's protection for the players, does this really interfere with your pursuit of life, liberty, and happiness? If it does you need therapy. Frankly, if I were at an event in Tel Aviv, I'd fully expect to hear a Jewish prayer; the same goes for a Hindu prayer in Bombay or a Muslim prayer in Damascus. And I wouldn't be offended, feel my rights were trampled, or be inclined to call a lawyer and whimper. I would be as respectful and tolerant of others and their right to express their beliefs as I expect them to be of me and mine. I would also have the right to ignore their prayer or pray in my own way during the time allotted. And since I would be in the minority, I would have the good sense to know my place and realize it is not the majority's job to make me happy.

Here's a fact that is considered politically incorrect and offensive to mention: Despite the unfounded celebration of multiculturism in this country, America is a nation founded on Christian principles, and continues to house a Christian majority. Check out your local phone book and compare the number of Christian churches to other religions and you'll grasp that America is still overwhelmingly Christian. And thus it seems perfectly reasonable that prayers said in school, at sporting events, military commencements, or in public in general would be Christian prayers; if someone has a problem with that, their sensitivity should not shut down the majority's right to worship. As a Christian, why must I be expected to tolerate the beliefs and freedom of worship of other faiths—or of their freedom not to worship—but meekly accept the fact that others shouldn't in turn be tolerant of my own freedom to worship as I see fit? And why should I buy into "separation of church and state" when it is never mentioned in our Constitution and has merely become a convenient way for atheists to exclude God from our everyday lives?

If you are offended or don't want to participate in a public prayer, you don't have to—just don't try to tell the rest of us that we can't do so. If a Christian tells you "Merry Christmas" and you find that offensive, or feel excluded because you don't recognize Christ, that's your problem, not the fault of the person who offered you their good wishes. You have the right to ignore the greeting just as they have the right to offer it. But do us all a favor and don't feel compelled to share your hurt feelings, because most of us could not care less. We have more important things to worry about in life than offending a few thin-skinned professional victims who think the populace should tiptoe through life in absolute dedication to making sure you're happy.

In fact, I'll make you a deal: Pray publicly—or choose not to pray at all—in a manner that supports your beliefs and I'll do the same, and we'll both agree that it's none of the other's business how, when, or where we talk to God. Fair enough? And, if, while a Christian prayer is being offered in public you find yourself feeling excluded, just ignore the prayer. Use the time to pray to your own god or to meditate—whatever gets you going. Just don't feel that it is your solemn duty to interfere with the freedom of worship others hold sacred and have fought for centuries to defend. My Bible tells me to pray without ceasing. It doesn't have disclaimers warning me to cease if it offends others.

Parting shot: If you disagree with this article or have found it offensive in any way you are free to dissent. However, don't feel compelled to share your feelings with me, because I don't care and you're not paying me to be your shrink. There was a time when I was more interested in feedback from disgruntled readers, but after authoring several books and hundreds of published articles I've developed a low threshold for whiners and crybabies who get triggered by something I write. If you feel so strongly about your views, instead of complaining about me, get busy and start your own web site, write your own books, author your own column, and find your own forum. The SendUsYourThoughts button following is reserved for those readers who have something positive to contribute.

This article brought an outpouring of affirmation and requests to reprint and distribute to friends, businesses, and churches. The fact that a business would take a stand for a clear religious issue was hailed far more than it was assailed, although we did hear from one unhappy and offended agnostic who complained that my "inane" remarks concerning Christianity bothered her and her daughter, who happened to be a witch. I was truly distraught to have upset such a charming family.

Example 2

Killed in Action: How You Can Help Their Survivors was written to create awareness and solicit help for the families of slain soldiers in Iraq and Afghanistan. I purposely placed it on our site one month before Christmas. The response we received from it was incredible. Many individuals and businesses alike rolled up their sleeves and donated to, raised money for, and adopted military families in order to support this worthy cause.

God & Country
Killed in Action: How You Can Help Their Survivors

Leaders always look for ways to impact and add value to others. Sometimes they do so directly by giving their time or expertise, and other times they give of their resources. During this festive season I want to share with you a way to do the latter and help some deserving families whose moms, dads, and spouses have given their lives for our nation. When you visit the web site www.killedinaction.com you will find an organization dedicated to helping the families of slain servicemen in Afghanistan and Iraq. A little-known fact is that when a soldier is killed in action his survivors get two things from the government: an American flag and a $12,000 insurance policy. That's it. In fact, until President Bush stepped in, the amount was just $6,000 and taxable. While the families of the 9-11 attacks were showered with streams of generosity, the survivors of the men and women fighting evil to keep us safer here at home get a pittance. Their kids can't go to college. Their spouses must often work two jobs while they take care of their kids just to make ends meet—and forget about prospering or enjoying many of the things we buy and take for granted every day, like a night out at your favorite restaurant or a weekend away.

At this web site you'll see how General Tommy Franks is involved in helping the Enduring Freedom KIA Fund, and you'll read about real heroes, killed while serving their country, and the struggles their survivors endure. One that touched me was the story of Joey Whitener, who had taken leave from Iraq to be with his wife for the birth of their son, Tristan. After returning to Iraq a few weeks later Joey was killed in an Apache helicopter crash, leaving his wife Beth and their newborn son to fend for themselves. Joey was 19. The memorial Beth wrote to him is at the site, as well as a picture of Joey holding Tristan. Unfortunately, there are many other stories and memorials at the site and it will grow each week while these men and women make the ultimate sacrifice. This Christmas season is going to be unbearable for their survivors, as they cope not only with their great loss of life but with financial worry and stress. Here are a few ideas that can help make a difference for these men and women and their children.

1. Tell your extended family (the aunts, uncles, and cousins who normally send gifts that end up at the bottom of a drawer in your closet) that in lieu of presents this year, you're asking they go to this site and make a donation in your name.
2. Make a personal donation at the web site. Any amount would be a great help.
3. E-mail this article to anyone you know who would have an interest in helping out.
4. Take up a collection in your workplace and send your donation in with a letter of thanks to the families of these men and women who are hurting, suffering, and need compassion.

When you hear on the news that the "501st" or "810th," or "1,056th" serviceman was killed in Iraq, that person is not just a number. They had a life. They had dreams. They had people they loved and who loved them back, and most of them were young—and left behind youthful and struggling families. While we can't bring back their loved ones we can help the families they left behind. Wouldn't you want others to do the same for you? As Americans we can and must help take care of our own. Charity begins at home. Thank you for considering how you may help, for taking action and for making a difference.

If you decide to do something to help, I'd appreciate hearing about it. Please let me know at the SendUsYourThoughts button that follows.

The SendUsYourThoughts button worked overtime on this article. Business owners took up collections in their workplaces and then matched the total amount given; others adopted military families, made small and substantial donations to the fund, and one client took out a full-page ad in their local newspaper and reprinted this article, which in turn multiplied the good exponentially, and another gave a $5,000 donation. Note: On Wednesday, May 11th, 2005 President Bush signed into law a provision that raised the $12,000 to $100,000, retroactive to October 7, 2001.

Example 3

Are You Just Making Money or Are You Making a Difference? was one of the first contributions to the God & Country section and was reprinted in publications worldwide. It still holds the record for the highest number of hits in the God & Country Section.

God & Country
Are You Just Making Money or
Are You Making a Difference?

Many friends and customers of LearnToLead know that best-selling author John Maxwell has been a major influence on my life. His leadership books and teachings are the foundation of my own business philosophy. John and I have been friends for many years, and I know that while many of you have read his works, you may not be fully aware of his heart.

And if you don't know John's heart then you don't know John at all.

John is the founder of a nonprofit organization called EQUIP. EQUIP provides leadership training and curricula to Christian leaders in some of the most inhospitable parts of the world. EQUIP teams are developing Christian leaders in India, the Middle East, Asia, Africa, and were recently in Iraq. Soon, EQUIP's trainers will embark across Europe and Latin America.

The benefactors of this training plant churches, recruit disciples, and spread the gospel of Jesus Christ in countries where Christians are a minority and oftentimes are persecuted. Every leader they teach covenants to train and mentor 25 additional leaders, while EQUIP supplies the structure, trainers, reinforcement, and training materials. EQUIP's major objective is to change the world by raising up 1,000,000 Christian leaders internationally by 2008. Yes, you read the number right: There are two commas and six zeros. EQUIP refers to this herculean effort as the Million Leaders Mandate; in launching this mammoth feat, John Maxwell and the EQUIP team members took a quantum leap from personal success to substantial significance.

Undoubtedly, this multiplication of Christian leaders and their subsequent influence will change the world politically, economically, and spiritually. The outcome of the Million Leaders Mandate will transcend success and create a legacy of eternal significance.

Speaking of significance, let's bring this to a more personal level: As a leader, are you just making money or are you making a difference? Are you consumed with success or striving towards significance? My hope is that it's the latter, because becoming merely successful isn't a good enough return on God's investment in your life. Perhaps you've experienced the emptiness of success. Strangely, attaining position and possessions often creates a letdown. It's like the child who, after all the hype and anticipation, opens his final present on Christmas morning and is stricken with the sinking feeling, "Is this all there is?" And while multitudes become successful financially and in their work, few live significant lives. In fact, when most people reflect upon their years on earth they will realize they did not live a significant life precisely because it was so easy to settle for a successful one. Sadly, when most people die it will be as though they never lived.

Frankly, this is inexcusable, because significance is within the grasp of everyone willing to embrace the right priorities. Contrary to what Hollywood promotes, it is not what you get or accumulate that makes you significant, but what you give away; what you contribute; the value you add to others, and what you become in the process.

Like many of you, my wife Rhonda and I give to charities. In fact, our company donates to charities ten percent of gross sales; not gross profit or net profit, but gross sales. Thus, when you spend $1,000 with us, $100 of it goes to various outreaches. This gives us far greater purpose than simply having a "job," makes running our business more exciting, and adds significance to even the smallest sale we make. We support causes ranging from prison ministries to local churches to Christian schools, but I can say truthfully that the money we invest in the work of EQUIP is the most significant, because it goes furthest in fulfilling the Great Commission: to bring the Gospel to every breathing soul on earth. Jesus said that if you want to find Him to look among the lost and that's exactly where EQUIP goes to fulfill the Million Leaders Mandate. While tepid souls wince at venturing into countries where simmering sentiment toward Westerners is escalating, EQUIP goes nonetheless, because lost people in these high-risk countries are not the enemy; they are the cause.

Soon, I begin a commitment to accompany an EQUIP team and teach Christian leadership principles 2 weeks annually for the next 3 years in Moscow. I'm humbled. I'm honored. I'm pumped and I'm ready. I'd go tomorrow if they'd let me.

Many of you are quite successful by worldly standards. You've worked hard and have gotten ahead of the pack, and may already serve worthy causes. If you're ready to take the next step from the personal success you've attained toward greater significance by reaching into the darkest corners of the globe and changing the world by raising up 1,000,000 Christian leaders by 2008, visit http://www.iequip.org to learn how you can help us, or give Doug Carter, Executive Vice-President of EQUIP, a call at 888-993-7847 and tell him I sent you. You'll love Doug. If I met the Devil and a cast of demons in a dark alley and could choose one man to be on my side it would be Doug Carter.

As a leader you, more than anyone, understand the power effective leadership has to affect change, maximize results, and manifest exponential growth. EQUIP is an organization founded by leaders, supported by leaders, with the mission to train and multiply 1,000,000 leaders by 2008. The time is short and we need a full-court press. I invite you to join us and hope to see you at an EQUIP event, a golf tour-

219

nament fundraiser, as a corporate sponsor on a donor's roster, or perhaps on an international trip, as we accomplish the Million Leaders Mandate together.

As the Million Leaders Mandate becomes reality the worldwide impact will be astounding. In the words of Samuel Logan Brengle, it will "confuse the Devil, astonish hell, rebuke unbelief and fill the world with light." What would it be worth to one day look your Maker in the eye and tell Him you helped make this happen?

Hoping this finds you ready to join us in the race.

Do you have the courage to make a difference?

Some people have such low self-esteem that they think of themselves as incapable of making a difference in the world. One "poor-pitiful-me-maudlin-misfit" remarked to me that perhaps if he were a famous politician or musician or actor that he would have the platform and financial wherewithal to make a difference. People who think this way need counseling. They see themselves as peons of society and think the right to make a difference resides in the "beautiful people" and higher beings living in Washington, D.C., or Hollywood. This is laughable. While it's not wise to generalize and stereotype vocations forgive me as I do, because politicians, actors, and musicians come as close to violating the conventional wisdom to not generalize than any other high-profile professions.

Think for a moment about how many politicians positively impact the society in which they live? How many really ever make a difference? And I'm not talking about the legacy of lies and deceit left by Nixon or the impact a Bill Clinton makes by leaving in his wake a culture of criminality, rationalization, and stained dresses in America. How many politicians make a *positive* difference? How many do more good than harm? Sadly, you probably won't need both hands to count the names of elected officials that make a significant positive difference during your lifetime.

Say Goodbye to Hollywood

What's even nuttier is the thought that most well-known actors or actresses use their fame and fortune to make a positive difference and leave the world better than they found it. Without a doubt, high-profile celebrity actors and actresses are the most overrated, overpaid people in the universe. For goodness sakes, these people put on makeup, read scripts, and play "make-believe" for a living. I'm not saying that many of them aren't talented. It's just that they're talented at reading scripts and playing make-believe! Get a grip!

There has never been a highly touted and high-profile group of people blessed with a worldwide platform and vast resources that have managed to remain as expendable to the betterment of humanity than the Hollywood horde. Just a generation or two ago these people were laughingstocks; unemployed misfits and outcasts who took up acting because it was the only thing they could do; read scripts—and the first actors didn't even have to do that.

While a handful of Hollywood-types consistently and substantially put others ahead of their own selfish agenda (Oprah Winfrey, Angelina Jolie, and Paul Newman are standouts in this regard) most have forgotten that with one very small exception, the world is made up of other people!

221

"To whom much is given much is required" doesn't seem to apply to this nest of narcissists, because in addition to being self-absorbed tightwads, many are just plain mean and nasty to the "common folk," and live their lives with the same moral soundness as Caligula. The fact that celebrities have fortune and fame shouldn't be allowed to justify the decadent way many of them live and treat others. In fact, their failure to use well the resources they've been blessed with should compound their condemnation. And what makes the majority of this crowd more repulsive is their lack of moral and patriotic values: Overwhelmingly, the Hollywood huddle is anti-anything that has to do with family values, God, or country.

To add to the hilarity of their world-class narcissism and the big deal these people make of themselves, the *People's Choice Awards* has now added categories for: "Best Smile," "Best Look," and "Best Hair." Give me a break! The on-slaught of "look at me and love me" award shows like *The Golden Globes, The Academy Awards, The Critics Choice Awards, The Emmy Awards, The Daytime Emmy Awards,* and *The People's Choice Awards* the Hollyweirds shower on themselves is mind-numbing, and the fact that so many viewers tune in to enable their self-worship is a national cry for help! America needs a shrink and millions of Americans need to get a life! The good news is that the ratings of these snore-fests have plummeted in recent years, befuddling Hollywood's as-sumption that they're the center of the universe for the rest of us.

On a positive note, actors and actresses have helped the economy by turning therapy and psychiatry into a booming growth industry. If the paparazzi hound them they feel abused, but when they're ignored they become suicidal. Go figure. Many of these people deserve your sympathy more than your admiration or envy. I could certainly include professional athletes in the category of overrated politicians, actors, actresses, and musicians, but many don't have the IQ to defend themselves.

How about musicians and the positive influence and impact they have on the world? Yes, every few years or so a group of musicians will band together to raise funds for a worthy cause, but these events are the exceptions and not the rule. Overall, their impact would have to be rated as a lot more bark than bite. In fact, the world witnessed how much clout Bruce Springsteen, James Taylor, John Mellencamp, REM, the Dixie Chicks, and the growing parade of activists made in the 2004 U.S. presidential election when they banded together and toured the country belching bile against President Bush. Ultimately, they made little difference in their endeavor to elect Senator Kerry, because most people could care less what simpletons who sing songs for a living think about the Patriot Act or Iraq. Did they have a right to do what they did? You bet they did. And regardless of which candidate you were for, you should give some credit to these musicians for having the guts to stick up for what they believed, even though they were unsuccessful in impacting the election's outcome.

While I watch very little television I do enjoy going to the movies and listening to music. But I keep the players in perspective and so should you. These folks are entertainers. They are there for your amusement and perform at your pleasure. Most do not have values worthy of envy, or lives worthy of emulation. Regardless of how rich or famous, these people still get morning breath, body odor, wrinkles, and grow old just like the poorest, most anonymous earthling.

What's the moral in my tirade? Stop selling yourself short and letting society's high-profile derelicts give you an inferiority complex. You have a better chance of making a difference right where you are, in your current capacity, fueled by a genuine passion, than most of these self-absorbed and decadent folks. It is absurd how many hard-working, honest, good-hearted, God-fearing men, women, and children would, should, or could even respect—much less admire—most of this human element, many of whom jumped into the gene pool while the lifeguard wasn't looking.

Hard-Charging Strategies

There is no question that *you* are capable of making a positive difference in the people around you, in your community, and in the world overall. The question is, are you willing to go to the trouble? For those of you who are, here are a few places you might begin and a few thoughts to get you started:

1. Support or sponsor a charity. Since you can't be everything to everyone and will never be able to support all the great causes that beckon for your time and dollars, narrow your focus. You can change charities from year to year as different causes tug at your heart-strings. Our organization gives 10 percent of our gross receipts to charities, including: Oprah Winfrey's Angel Network, Christ Prison Fellowship Ministries, EQUIP (men-

tioned earlier in this chapter), Voice of the Martyrs, The Center for Reclaiming America, Children Inc., Love in the Name of Christ, Killed in Action Fund (mentioned earlier in this chapter), churches, and others. Over and above the 10 percent we contribute to several political organizations that promote the values we embrace.

Suffice it to say, there is no shortage of outlets to park your time or money. Choose the ones that share your values and reflect your heart. I do suggest you ask some questions about how they use the money and where it goes. I've stopped giving to the United Way because many of their chapters have cut off hundreds of thousands of dollars to the Boy Scouts of America. The reason? The Scouts object to homosexuals being allowed to lead these young boys as scoutmasters, and gay lobbyists retaliated by convincing the United Way to cut off their funding. Any organization that buckles under to this type of pressure is no longer worthy of our dollars. The NFL should reexamine their support for a group like the United Way that punishes and penalizes an organization like the Scouts, where many of the NFL's own players learned leadership and responsibility.

By the way, you don't always have to donate money to make a difference—you can give of your time. One of the most rewarding things my wife ever did was to assume a route and each week deliver meals to shut-ins through the Meals-on-Wheels program.

2. Use your web site for community service purposes. Feature links to local or national charities that your organ-

ization supports. You can also use this "community works" section to broadcast your own involvement in local community or charitable endeavors. And you do so not to boast, but to create awareness and encourage others to get involved as well.

3. Support political candidates who exemplify your values. When it comes to elections, either put up or shut up. Start to get involved in local and national issues that reflect your values and affect you and your family; this goes beyond showing up on voting day to punch the button. Even society's knaves can manage to pull this one off. And don't sit by idly and cry out the excuse that you don't like "politics." This is just a rationalization for laziness and indifference. There are nut jobs running for office in every election that can drastically impact your business, your lives, and your children. Getting involved in your democracy is one of your greatest privileges and also one of your greatest protections. Don't be an ignorant whiner who sits on the sidelines and then complains when the "wrong guy" wins.

The Internet makes researching a candidate's views simple and makes donating to their campaigns quick and easy. Even though we live in California, via the Internet we were able to get involved with and support key congressional candidates in Kentucky, South Dakota, and Illinois during a recent national election.

4. Mentor someone on the job and have them pay it forward. What if you're broke and don't have the money to

give, and are so busy at work there's not time available, either—so what are you to do? Mentor a high-potential employee on the job as outlined in Chapter 3 and have him or her pay it forward to one of his or her high potentials. You can always impact the world by positively impacting others.

5. Live by example for your kids. Want to leave the world better than you found it? Then start by nurturing the human capital that sleeps under your roof each night. Realize that the best gift you can give to a loved one is not material. Instead, it is your focused attention. Too many businesspeople give all they have at work; once they get home they're out of gas, and maintain their relationships with mere emotional leftovers.

Give your spouse and kids the focused attention required to make a real difference in their lives. Shut up for a while and listen for a change. The key to having more influence with them is to open yourself up to being influenced, because once they feel understood they will be more willing to understand the thoughts or advice you have for them. And remember that it's not all about you. The only way to have strong, fulfilling relationships at home is to put others first. Even if you're the big boss at work, your spouse is an equal partner in your lives together. This is not a relationship you can micromanage or become too demanding with. One of the first questions you must ask and answer when you wake up each morning is, "What can I do today to make my spouse's day better?" If you want more from your relationships with others you must start by giving, not taking. Positively impact the people that mean the most to you and you will make a difference in the world.

An additional payoff of becoming more effective in your relationships at home is that the resulting sense of fulfillment and esteem will follow you right back into the workplace and make you even more effective on the job. You need more than quality time at home; you need quantity time as well. But the only way you get quantity time at home is if you become more effective at work and don't have to spend as much time there.

6. Start small. Don't let the news stories about windbags like Ted Turner pledging 1 billion dollars to the United Nations (the biggest waste of philanthropy in world history) psyche you out and think the little bit you can do won't matter. It's estimated that the nation's richest 1 percent—who own two-fifths of U.S. wealth—donate just 2 percent of their incomes each year, versus 6 percent for families in the bottom income bracket. Fully 20 percent of the wealthiest estates leave absolutely nothing. These Scrooges are to be pitied, because what they don't realize—and you can only experience this if you give cheerfully and from the heart—is that the rewards to your mental and spiritual health, self-esteem, and overall sense of worth you gain by taking your eyes off your own pathetic problems and ailments and shifting them to others is priceless.

7. Drop the excuses. Oftentimes I'll hear some lamebrain mumble, "When I have more money I'll be able to give." That's not how it works. Giving starts the receiving process. You give first. If you can't give $10.00 off a $100 in-

come do you expect anyone to believe you're going to give $10,000 from a $100,000 income? How or whether you give often depends on how you see yourself. If you're absorbed in self-pity and think the world hasn't done enough to make you happy you'll become an entitled scourge of a brat who drains society rather than edifies it. But if you see yourself as a leader, a pacesetter, and a catalyst for good, then you'll become an unstoppable force wherever you happen to reside and with whatever you happen to do for a living. After all, it's not what you do but *how* you do what you do that determines much of your success and satisfaction in life.

8. Fade the heat. As I mentioned at the outset of this chapter, this final strategy will take the most courage of all. You will make some waves. But if you remember that your job is not to make everyone happy; if you'll embrace that you have an obligation to leave the world better than you found it, and when you resolve to never cower and trade your values for valuables, doing the right thing is easy.

Final Word from the Author

At the beginning of this book I set out two key objectives, made one promise, one request, and one demand:

The two objectives
1. Show indisputable evidence of how political correctness in society diminishes the way you run your business and deal with your employees.

2. Provide hard-charging strategies and the inspiration to buck the politically correct trend and lead at an ultimate level of effectiveness, in spite of the PC stench.

The promise
I would not pull any punches and would present the material in the most direct and brutally honest manner in which I am capable. I even admitted I would cross the line from time to time to make my point.

The request
I requested that you keep an open mind as you read the book and asked that even if you didn't agree with something that you would at least think about it. And then if you still didn't like it, to move on and find something that would work for you.

The demand
I told you that I was not interested in hearing that I offended you, hurt your feelings, or otherwise ruffled your feathers. Let there be no misunderstanding that I still mean what I wrote.

I have done my best to deliver on the promises I made in the Preface and Introduction. If you don't see the relevance that society's march off the politically correct cliff has on your business; on relations with your employees and your own self-esteem, and if you haven't walked away with the tools necessary to combat the madness, then there is little hope for you as a leader. Unfortunately, you also wasted your hard-earned money on this book. It will be just a matter of time before you are chewed up, spit out, and rendered totally irrelevant in the workplace. In fact, you may already be at that point. If not, the clock is ticking and before long it will strike midnight.

The strategies in this book are not complicated but they take courage, resolve, and a shift in attitude. They require discipline, a new definition of fairness, and a commitment, rather than merely an interest to build an elite organization. Do you have the right stuff? Only time will tell. I'm pulling for you, but there's nothing anyone else can do to help you at this point. You will either decide to lead or be led; stretch others to your standards or be dragged down to theirs; stand for something bold and great or fall for everything in general; do what is right or take the wimp's way out by doing what is cheap, easy, popular, and convenient. I hope you make the right decision: to be a politically incorrect and principled leader and to make the waves necessary to build and sustain your success.

At the risk of sounding negative I will tell you that the odds are against you. Most people will not find the "right stuff" within them to go against the politically correct tide. I hope you are the exception, because right now the world is crying out for your leadership; it needs you. If you're up to the task then put this book down, stand and deliver.

Notes

Chapter 1

1. Donald T. Phillips, *Lincoln on Leadership* (New York: Warner Books, 1992) 131.
2. Ibid., 7.
3. Ibid., 134.
4. John Wooden with Jack Tobin, *They Call Me Coach* (Chicago: Contemporary Books, 1988) 12.
5. John Wooden with Steve Jamison, *Wooden* (Chicago: Contemporary Books, 1997) 115.
6. Gary George, *Winning is a Habit* (New York: HarperCollins, 1997) 74.
7. Ibid., 75.
8. Ibid., 72.

Chapter 2

1. Mark Krikorian, *National Review Magazine: Amnesty, Again* (New York: National Review, Inc. January 16, 2004) 30.
2. Victor David Hanson, *National Review Magazine: California, Here They Come (and Come)* (New York: National Review, Inc. August 11, 2003) 30.
3. Stephen Moore, *National Review Magazine: Arnold's New Role* (New York: National Review, Inc. January 26, 2004) 22.

Chapter 3

1. Heather MacDonald, *City Journal: L'affaire Blair* (New York: as printed in *FrontPageMagazine.com*, May 14, 2003).
2. Cliff Kincaid, *Accuracy in Media: Diversity Scandal Rocks New York Times* (Washington, D.C.: as printed in *FrontPageMagazine.com*, May 12, 2003).
3. Ann Coulter, *FrontPageMagazine.com: Lies, the New York Times, and the Little Matter of Race* (Los Angeles, *FrontPageMagazine.com*, May 22, 2003).
4. Jim Collins, *Good to Great* (New York: Harper Collins, 2001) 16.

5. Lou Gerstner, *Who Says Elephants Can't Dance?* (New York: HarperCollins, 2002) as reprinted in (Concordia, Pennsylvania: Soundview *Executive Book Summaries*, March 2003) 2.

Chapter 4

1. Oren Harari, *The Leadership Secrets of Colin Powell* (New York: McGraw Hill, 2002) 17.
2. George, *Winning is a Habit*, 125.
3. Ibid., 86.
4. Ibid., 78.
5. *New King James Version Holy Bible* (Nashville, TN: Thomas Nelson Publishers, 1992) Matthew 23:25.
6. Ibid., Luke 14: 8-12.
7. Ibid., Luke 14: 12-14.
8. Alan Axelrod, *Patton on Leadership* (Paramus, NJ: Prentice Hall, 1999) 24.

Chapter 5

1. Rev. Jesse Lee Peterson, *Scam* (Nashville, TN: Wind Books, 2003) 34.
2. Ibid.
3. Ibid.
4. Ibid., 35.
5. B. Forrest Clayton, *Suppressed History* (Cincinnati, OH: Armistead Books, 2003) 23.
6. Ibid., 25.
7. Anne Coulter, *Slander* (New York: Crown Publishers, 2002) 156.
8. Ibid.
9. Ibid.
10. Ibid.

Chapter 6

1. Daniel J. Flynn, *Why the Left Hates America* (New York: Forum, 2002) 68.
2. Ibid., 18.

Chapter 8

1. Lieutenant Colonel Robert "Buzz" Patterson, *Dereliction of Duty* (Washington, D.C.: Regnery Publishing, 2003) 4.
2. *New King James Version Holy Bible*, I Corinthians 15:33.
3. Ibid., Proverbs 13:20.
4. Wooden, *Wooden*, 153.
5. James M. Strock, *Reagan on Leadership* (Rocklin, CA: Prima Publishing, 1998).

Bibliography

Axelrod, Alan. (1999). *Patton on Leadership.* Paramus, NJ: Prentice Hall.

Collins, Jim. (2001). *Good to Great.* New York: HarperCollins.

Coulter, Ann. (2002). *Slander.* New York: Crown.

Coulter, Ann. (2003). *Lies, the* New York Times, *and the Little Matter of Race.* Retrieved May 22, 2003, from www.FrontPageMagazine.com.

Clayton, Forrest B. (2003). *Suppressed History.* Cincinnati, OH: Armistead.

Flynn, Daniel J. (2002). *Why the Left Hates America.* New York: Forum.

George, Gary. (1997). *Winning is a Habit.* New York: HarperCollins.

Gerstner, Lou. (2002). *Who Says Elephants Can't Dance?* New York: Harper-Collins.

Hanson, Victor David. (2003). California, here they come (and come). *National Review Magazine, 15,* 30.

Harari, Oren. (2002). *The Leadership Secrets of Colin Powell.* New York: McGraw Hill.

Kincaid, Cliff. (2003). *Accuracy in media: Diversity scandal rocks New York Times.* Retrieved May 12, 2003, from www.FrontPageMagazine.com.

Krikorian, Mark. (2004). Amnesty, again. *National Review Magazine, 15,* 29–30.

MacDonald, Heather. (2003). *City Journal: L'affaire Blair.* Retrieved May 14, 2003, from www.FrontPageMagazine.com.

Moore, Stephen. (2004). Arnold's New Role. *National Review Magazine, 16,* 22.

New King James Version Holy Bible. (1992). Nashville, TN: Thomas Nelson.

Patterson, Robert. (2003). *Dereliction of Duty.* Washington, D.C.: Regnery Publishing.

Peterson, Jesse Lee. (2003). *Scam.* Nashville, TN: Wind Books.

Phillips Donald T. (1992). *Lincoln on Leadership.* New York: Warner.

Strock, James M. (1998). *Reagan on Leadership.* Rocklin, CA: Prima.

Wooden, John, & Tobin, Jack. (1988). *They Call Me Coach.* Chicago: Contemporary Books.

Wooden, John with Jamison, Steve. 1997. *Wooden.* Chicago: Contemporary Books.

About the Author

Dave **Anderson** is president of Dave Anderson's LearnToLead, an international sales and management training organization. He has run some of the most successful automotive retail dealerships in America. He is a business columnist and speaker, presenting at 150 engagements annually. He has authored *Selling Above the Crowd: 365 Strategies for Sales Excellence*, *No-Nonsense Leadership*, and *Up Your Business*, as well as numerous CD and DVD training programs. Dave is a member of the National Speaker's Association. His web site, www.learntolead.com, provides hundreds of free sales, management, and leadership training articles. Dave resides in California with his wife and daughter.